SEEKING TO SERVE

The Legacy of Seattle's Plymouth Congregational Church

SEEKING TO SERVE

The Legacy of Seattle's Plymouth Congregational Church

Mildred Tanner Andrews

K H
Kendall/Hunt
Publishing Company
Dubuque, Iowa

Library of Congress Catalog Card Number: 88–81288

ISBN 0–8403–4761–8

Printed in the United States of America
10 9 8 7 6 5 4 3 2 1

This account of the legacy of Plymouth Congregational Church is dedicated to the nearly 10,000 people who have built and sustained the congregation.

This project was made possible by the special gifts of

The Page Ballard family in memory of Page and Pat Ballard

Frederick V. Betts in memory of Arline E. Betts

The Russell M. Bird estate

Anne F. and Howard E. Conkle in memory of Gordon P. Conkle and his paternal grandparents, Katherine W. and Frank P. Conkle

Marion Fish Cox in memory of William Edward Cox

Margaret W. Evenson in memory of William E. Evenson

Ellen Morford Fisher and Donald Fisher in memory of Gertrude Smith Morford and Kenneth Morford; Ellen Hubbard Smith, Margaret McPherson Smith, and James Van Alen Smith; Frederick Hubbard; and Caroline Burr Smith and Eben Smith

Missy and Ken Fisher

Erna Frank in memory of William E. Frank

Margie and John Gibson in tribute to Louise and Martin Goslin

Bertha Graham in memory of William E. Graham

The Gruger family in memory of William Sallada and Harriet Hart Gruger

Evelyn L. Gunther in memory of Julius J. Gunther

Jane I. and Joseph W. Hall in memory of Felix M. and Lucile F. Davis, and Fred S. and Sylvia J. Hall

Helena and Dickinson Harper

Bruce R. Hildebrand, David B. Hildebrand, and Susan Hildebrand Lepp in tribute to Robert B. Hildebrand

Beatrice Selby Hokamp in memory of Herbert Frederick Hokamp

Esther and Al Instebo in tribute to Elsie and Dwight Cart

Helen and Al Lilygren

Frances P. Owen

Leona Schnaidt in memory of Herbert J. Schnaidt and Sarah Black Rataichak

Grace Smith in tribute to Harold V. Smith

Sarah Morford Tousley and Russell Tousley in memory of Gertrude Smith Morford and Kenneth Morford; Ellen Hubbard Smith, Margaret McPherson Smith, and James Van Alen Smith; Frederick Hubbard; and Carrie Burr Smith and Eben Smith

Marion J. Waller and Peggy Anne Jacobsson in memory of Harry E. and Jessie W. Jacobsson and Marion J. Waller in memory of Harold H. Waller

A Plymouth member in memory of Mary Skelton

Contents

Foreword

It seems to me a non sequitur that I should write a foreword to this historical narrative of the life of Plymouth Congregational Church, United Church of Christ, Seattle, Washington, in the year 1988. More in keeping would be my writing an afterword. I belong at the end of the story and not at the beginning. After five years of sharing Plymouth's ministry, I am still in the process of being initiated into the life of this congregation.

Nevertheless, I am particularly conscious that it is very much "the legacy" of Plymouth Church which I have inherited. The title of this volume aptly indicates that we who now participate in this congregation have received an immeasurable gift from those who have gone before us. The relationship among the past, the present, and the future is one of those intriguing theological enigmas. We can never start at the beginning. We are always the inheritors of a tradition. Our Plymouth past continues to be very much alive among us. Our legacy has enabled us to sustain the vision of a gathered people who are both formidable and flexible as we live out our destiny in this city.

I came to Plymouth in September of 1983. Donna and I left our rooted lives in Massachusetts because we responded enthusiastically to the challenge of ministry in this congregation. As we made our way 3,000 miles across the United States, we read to each other in the car *The Path We Came By*, the earlier history of Plymouth written by Alice Rayner in 1937.

This updated telling of the Plymouth story is decidedly more accurate in that Mildred Andrews has appropriately highlighted the importance of lay as well as clergy leadership. To my mind, lay leadership is the most significant reality in the continuing effectiveness of this congregation. This new volume is clearly a collection of personal tributes to the almost 10,000 people who have shared the life of Plymouth Church.

In addition to the author, two other persons have contributed time and energy beyond calculation to the creation of this book. They are Judy Pickens and John Gibson. We are indebted to them in particular for seeing this project to completion. They have thus added to the legacy that now belongs to all who read this story.

To read it is to be reminded afresh that no one inherits a legacy without taking on the obligations of faithful stewardship. The gift is not for wasting nor for self-indulgence. The inheritance is for sustaining the ongoing ministry of this people whom we call Plymouth Church.

Joseph C. Williamson
Seattle, Washington
Eastertide 1988

Preface and Acknowledgments

In the fall of 1989, Plymouth Congregational Church marks its 120th anniversary as a major congregation in downtown Seattle. It was founded within months of the incorporation of Seattle, and this milestone anniversary coincides with the centennial of Washington State.

Although historians have written extensively about Seattle, few have taken into account the impact of its churches. This book is a history of one Seattle church in the context of the growth and development of its city. Through the years, Plymouth has been a primary source of nurturance to its people, "refueling" and informing them so that they can express their religious convictions by collective and individual service to the community.

For the members of Plymouth, this book is the story of their life as a congregation. For members of the denomination and other religious bodies, it is an account of church expansion and ecumenism. For others with an interest in local or urban legacies, it is a fresh perspective on more general studies.

In 1985 when members of Plymouth's Church Council voted to undertake this project, they decided to place its history in a larger social context. As an outside historian, I have found researching and writing about Plymouth both challenging and enlightening; I was previously unaware of the significant role the church had played in Seattle's development.

Because of the complexities of this story, I often encountered differing points of view in personal interviews and other research. When opinions varied, I tried to include diverse views and have sometimes offered my own interpretation. The text attempts to reclaim the substantial contributions of women to Plymouth's heritage and uses their own names whenever they could be determined. Their titles are in keeping with usage of the time. I have cited sources in the text, without additional annotation, when the information is from the Plymouth archives or from personal interviews.

I have enjoyed writing this book, partially because of the wealth of material but especially because of the many talented, caring, and stimulating people who have helped me. I am grateful to the Plymouth members, past and present clergy, and associates in the community who generously shared their recollections. I am particularly indebted to the editorial committee: Frances Owen with her knowledge of Plymouth and the community, John Haigh with his career experience as a reporter and editor for *The Seattle Times*, and Judy Pickens with her expertise in inclusive language. She coordinated the committee, edited the manuscript, and supervised publication of this book.

In addition to critical reviews by committee members and past and present clergy, the manuscript benefits from lay reviewers Vivian Bowden, Mildred Clark, Ginny Ean, Margie Gibson, Jack Griswold, Ann Sandstrom, and Janet Steputis. I also had the pleasure of working with Myrtle Pedersen and her crew in the church's historical room. They shared their love for Plymouth and steered me to treasured memories in the archives.

Harold Smith was among earlier members of the congregation who recorded their own anecdotes and interpretations of events. Following his retirement in 1961 as church business manager, he chronicled historical highlights made available to this project by his wife, Grace. Alice Rayner in 1937 wrote *The Path We Came By*, a book rich in detail about Plymouth's early years. As contemporary sources, I am grateful to the current staff for their perspectives on the church's more recent history.

Finally, my personal thanks to my husband, George, for his unstinting encouragement of my efforts.

Mildred Tanner Andrews
Seattle, Washington
April 1988

Plymouth stands today—as it has for 120 years—in the heart of Seattle.

Introduction

From Seattle's early history to the present, the people of Plymouth Congregational Church have been empowered by their faith and fellowship to address social concerns in the community. Whether their route to the church took them over dirt roads, wood-plank streets, or modern freeways, Plymouth people have throughout the decades steadfastly maintained this mission.

Today's Plymouth is an architecturally striking building, contemporary but unmistakably a place of worship. It nestles in a forest of towering office buildings and hotels, drawing members from all parts of the greater metropolitan area. While its neighbors thrive on materialistic competition, the church draws life from the human face of the city.

This home is the fourth for Plymouth, always in downtown Seattle. The church has been part of the myriad of physical and social changes that have propelled this toehold on the Western frontier into its current status as a major regional and international center. The congregation officially dates from October 1869, the same year that the Washington Territorial Legislature granted the city a charter.

Plymouth's roots extend to the arrival of the first white settlers in November 1851. That party's leader, Arthur Armstrong Denny, and his wife, Mary, cleared land overlooking Elliott Bay and built a home on what is now premium property in downtown Seattle. In line with other Protestants of many denominations, they pledged their support when Seattle's first minister, a Methodist, arrived in 1854. Fifteen years later when local Congregationalists began to organize, several Dennys were among the townsfolk who switched their allegiance to the new church.

Like this influential family, other early Plymouth people are deeply enmeshed in Seattle history. James Colman's shipping business flourished from the Colman Dock on the central waterfront where commuters now board the state ferries.

Hiram Chittenden's locks connect Lake Union with Puget Sound. James Moore's opulent downtown theater still draws crowds.

Oliver and Mary Shorey figured prominently in the early days of the University of Washington. He carved the elaborate balustrade and classic Doric columns for the main building of the territorial university, and she was the first matron of the dormitory. John Denny (Arthur's father) successfully lobbied in Washington, D.C., for siting of the school in Seattle. He was chairman of the Territorial Legislature's education committee and was, no doubt, boosted in his cause by having previously served with Abraham Lincoln in the Illinois Legislature. Arthur Denny introduced the bill that in early 1861 formalized the siting decision and then donated his 10-acre knoll for the campus.

In their commitment to education, the university's founders struck a familiar chord in Congregationalism's history. The denomination had by then already established several of what would become major independent colleges (including Harvard, Yale, Mount Holyoke, and Whitman). At the same time, Congregationalists promoted a government-supported system of free public education.

These community leaders and the many others whose names are not so well known have drawn strength and direction from Plymouth to improve their city and respond to more-distant needs. This account spans some 120 years of their witness, from the handful of Congregationalists who established the church through the thousands who, over the decades, have been attracted to it.

In more than literal terms, Plymouth is grounded in its city. In seeking to serve, this church has informed and enabled its people to act for justice, nurture one another through the trauma of war and social uncertainty, and foster broad-based ecumenical cooperation. Here is the story of that grounding and its legacy to Seattle.

1

In the Beginning 1869–1890

In the late 1860s, Seattle already had the layout of a city destined for commercial success and regional leadership. Front Street skirted the waterfront, and rutted dirt roads traversed precipitous hills and muddy tide flats to form blocks platted in a semblance of modern-day downtown.

John and Caroline Sanderson were determined to add to this landscape. As direct descendants of Mayflower Pilgrims, they believed that Seattle should have a piece of Plymouth Rock. That piece would grow, somewhat fitfully, over the next 20 years into a church that not only survived but also helped extend the reach of Congregationalism and add a strong voice to the stance of good citizens against frontier vices.

Seattle's population of nearly 1,000 was mostly comprised of single men who had ventured West in search of freedom, fortune, or the elusive ideal home. Although the native Salish had moved to nearby reservations, many still worked in Seattle. They felled trees and slid them down the "skid road" to Yesler's mill, sold seafood and baskets on the streets, and conducted a lively trade with local merchants.

In 1869, city founders induced the Territorial Legislature to grant Seattle a charter, whereupon mill owner Henry Yesler was elected the first mayor. Citizens unhesitatingly voted to levy taxes for street improvements and a $2,500, two-story Central School.

The Fledgling Church

Another event of 1869 was the organization of the Plymouth

Congregational Society. By early the next year, it would become Plymouth Congregational Church.

Prior to this time, the only houses of worship in town were the "brown church" (Methodist Protestant) and the "white church" (Methodist Episcopal). The Catholics were ably shepherded by Father F. X. Prefontaine and were planning their building. The Episcopalians were organized and would have a building in 1870. Whether more churches were needed or even supportable in the small town was questionable. Each denomination—Episcopalian, Presbyterian, and Congregationalist—wanted its own identity, however, and adherents were busily canvassing their neighbors in search of soulmates.

On October 16, 1869, Mr. Sanderson called to order a meeting at the "little building on the hill, known as the County Court House" for the purpose of organizing the Plymouth Congregational Society. Joining him as subscribers to the constitution were Stephen Pearl Andrews, William S. Baxter, A. N. Merrick, J. T. Jordan, Dr. George V. Calhoun, D. R. Lord, C. P. Stone, and the Reverend John F. Damon, whom the group elected as its pastor.

According to the Reverend Dr. Samuel Greene who came to Washington Territory in 1874 to manage early Congregational missionary work, Plymouth's founders were "for the most part businessmen who truly believed that the life and character of the community would be greatly bettered and improved, should the proposed church become a fact and a recognized institution of the growing town. Doubtless they knew, certainly some did, what churches gathered under the Congregational plan had done for other communities and could do for this one."

In these pioneer days when new denominations were competing to survive, parishioners frequently switched their allegiance. Later that winter the same Mr. Andrews who was a subscriber at Plymouth's constitutional meeting recorded the minutes of Seattle First Baptist Church where he was to become a leading member.

Under Mr. Damon's leadership, the Plymouth Congregational Society immediately instituted Sunday meetings in what was known as "Yesler's Hall," a large room above Kellogg's

The Reverend John F. Damon was Plymouth's first minister (1869–1872). He was also then deputy grand master of the Grand Masonic Lodge of Washington Territory.

Drug Store at Mill and Commercial streets. Within a week of its organization, the group had expanded to the point at which, with five teachers and 20 scholars, it could begin Sunday school work.

In an 1892 historical sketch, Mr. Sanderson described the early Sunday school as long on frontier ingenuity and short on theologically trained staff or published materials: "There were no singing book papers or lesson leaves, but enthusiasm prevailed and a friendly spirit was shown by other denominations. Singing books were loaned by Mr. Hiram Burnett from the Episcopal Sunday School which convened at a different hour and money was soon raised to purchase the other helps. Before long it became evident that a regular church organization was necessary both to obtain missionary aid and to make more permanent the fast growing work."

Prior to the founding of Plymouth, the Washington Territory had only one Congregational church: the parish across the Cascades in Walla Walla. It was organized in 1865 by pioneer missionaries the Reverend Cushing Eells and the Reverend P. B. Chamberlain; the latter became its first minister. Because of geographic barriers, the two churches had little opportunity for fellowship in their early years. The Sandersons and other founders of Plymouth had visited the First Congregational Church in San Francisco, the largest Congregational parish on the West Coast. They logically chose it as Plymouth's mother church because of this familiarity and the fact that marine trade already connected the two communities.

Thus, only three months after the initial meeting, a group of Congregationalists—this time including women—met at the Sanderson home, a wide-verandahed white house set in an orchard just north of what is now the Smith Tower. In his meticulous, flowing script, Plymouth's first clerk, George Farley, recorded what transpired:

> At a meeting of those wishing to form a Congregational Church in the town of Seattle, Washington Territory, there did convene at the home of John H. Sanderson upon Friday evening, January 14, 1870, the following named persons, to wit: Rev. J. F. Damon, John H. Sanderson, John W. Denny, George E. Farley, Caroline M. (Mrs. John H. Sanderson), Mary R. (Mrs. John W. Denny), who did then proceed as follows: after prayer, the Confession of Faith and Covenant of the First Congregational Church of San Francisco, California, was read and unanimously adopted as the Confession of Faith and Covenant of the Plymouth Congregational Church of Seattle, Washington Territory.[1]

On January 16, 1870, Mr. Damon conducted the first worship service in Yesler's Hall. According to the clerk's minutes, "The members made public confession of their faith and partook of the first communion."

The founders viewed their membership as a very serious commitment. Along with avowing their faith in God, they re-

1. George E. Farley, Minutes of the Plymouth Congregational Society, Oct. 16, 1869, Plymouth archives.

The congregation's first worship service was in Yesler's Hall above this store.

pented by professing sorrow for their sins and "renouncing them forever." Each promised to be a true disciple of Christ "in the sanctuary, in the family, and in the closet and in every situation and relation of life." They committed to attend Plymouth's "meetings for prayer, its public worship and its Sacraments, in love and charity with its members, conscientiously laboring to promote its purity, peace, union and edification."

For a frontier town, attendance was remarkable, averaging 100 at both morning and evening services. The charismatic Mr. Damon (who had also trained as an attorney) may have been partially responsible. Historian Alice Rayner says: "He was a fluent speaker, skilled at playing upon the emotions of his hearers. There was never a dry eye at his funerals, and he was equally in demand for weddings. Was in fact known up and down the Sound as the 'marrying parson.' "[2]

In March the congregation moved its place of worship to

2. Alice E. Rayner, *The Path We Came By: A History of Plymouth Congregational Church* (Seattle, 1937), 18.

Yesler's new Pavilion on Front Street, which had better lighting but was poorly heated. The Rayner history notes that services at times had to be cancelled—once because of the intense cold, on other occasions because the Pavilion was undergoing repairs, and on the evening of July third "to permit decoration for the morrow." During the week, the Pavilion was used for all sorts of public gatherings, including many that were not condoned by the church. Prior to Sunday morning, someone always had to sweep up the sawdust that was strewn across the floor to absorb the inevitable tobacco juice from Saturday night.

Request for Funding Assistance

In the spring of 1870, the congregation conducted its first pledge drive and requested denominational assistance. Church officers John Sanderson, John Denny, and George Farley wrote a letter to the American Home Missionary Association that reads in part:

> The undersigned . . . would respectfully ask for aid from the A.H.M. Society, to enable us to make up a salary of one thousand dollars ($1000) in gold for our pastor elect, Rev. John F. Damon, an ordained minister, (and) member of the Congregational Association of Oregon . . . who has been laboring in our midst since October of last year, and under whose charge a church organization was perfected January 16, 1870, from which time we desire his commission to date. We pledge, and have made arrangements by subscription to secure the sum of Four Hundred Dollars in gold, and believe that it will promote the cause of Christ in this region . . . (Mr. Damon) is engaged in no other calling than the Gospel ministry, and depends entirely thereupon for support. . . . We would respectfully request a generous recognition and prompt forwarding of at least half of the sum asked for from January 16, would relieve him from serious embarrassment, and promote an influence in the community, which even now appears to be for the good . . .

The requested funds were forthcoming, and Mr. Damon

took seriously his position, extending his mission throughout Puget Sound. On alternate Monday evenings he preached at Port Gamble and Port Madison and on other occasions at Port Blakely and Port Ludlow.

During his first year on Puget Sound, he wrote to the Reverend Dr. Milton Badger of the American Home Missionary Association that he had traveled 3,700 miles "on direct routes of missionary labor," despite chronic bronchitis and severe fever, and had "totally exhausted my own financial resources." Because his physician had since ordered him to confine his work to Seattle, he stressed the potential of Congregationalism in the area and pleaded for "all the money you can spare" and additional pastoral support to extend "the Redeemer's Kingdom."

Mr. Damon repeatedly extolled the virtues of the members of his congregation, juxtaposing them against the town's unsavory characters. In one of his letters he wrote: "While the sentiment of our more permanent residents is as healthy as anyplace, the floating, homeless, idle population requires the best effort of every moral man and woman to subdue the depravity that scarcely seeks the cover of darkness for its deeds." Noting that the eagerly awaited transcontinental railroad would infuse the area with a huge population increase, he stressed the urgency of a business community with moral power. He also emphasized that Seattle's wealth would grow so that Plymouth would no longer need aid from the association.

When she later reminisced about this bleak and uncertain period, early member Cassandra E. George told how Plymouth's very survival was tested and how the congregation rallied to face its future: "The Presbyterians had no church building, and they were as few and impecunious as ourselves. In a spirit of common helplessness we began to look toward each other. I do not know who made the first overtures, but a committee of three was appointed from each to confer with a view of uniting forces." At the close of the meeting, Plymouth's delegation rejected any further thought of a merger because the Presbyterians "proposed to furnish the preacher. . . ."

In their effort to absorb the Congregationalists, the Presbyterians went so far as to request that the Portland-based Congregational Home Missionary Association of Oregon and Washington disband Plymouth Church. Mrs. George quoted the Reverend Dr. George Atkinson's reply: "I have no authority to disband this church, and should disbandment take place, it might defeat the possibility of any further attempt at building up Congregational work on Puget Sound."

Because their temporary quarters in Yesler's Pavilion were so unsatisfactory, the members soon came to the conclusion that they would have to secure a lot and build their own church. Everyone assisted with the fund-raising. As Mrs. George recalled: "Our women were master hands at making comforts and other needle-craft, and we gave suppers in Yesler's Hall."

While the trustees concerned themselves with securing his salary, Mr. Damon made a springtime trip to San Francisco to request assistance from other churches. In an 1871 letter to the American Home Missionary Association, he stated that the funds would "enable the purchase of a suitable building lot for the erection of an edifice dedicated and exclusively devoted to the worship of the Almighty God."

During the summer, the young church continued to attract new members and visitors, including several from up and down the Sound who came to Seattle for weekends. One of the visitors was Captain S. O. Whitmore of Port Ludlow who, reportedly wanting to make a favorable impression on one of the young women in the congregation, contributed $10 in gold toward the purchase of a pump organ. Despite this self-serving motive, Captain Whitmore's gift made a fine impression on the grateful congregation. The arrival of the organ from San Francisco was indeed a memorable event, with an enthusiastic throng crowding the Pavilion to hear Fannie Russell play and to join the church quartet in song.

Plymouth's First Home

In the fall of 1871, Mr. Damon was forced to resign because

The Territorial University building standing atop Arthur Denny's knoll is distinguished by its fluted cupola. The school's first campus was near the site of today's Four Seasons Olympic Hotel. At left in this Ashel Curtis photo is Plymouth Church at Second Avenue and Spring Street and at right is the Methodist Protestant Church. (Courtesy University of Washington Photography Collection)

of failing health. The congregation persevered with the help of interim pastors and more than doubled in membership to nearly 90 souls. At the same time, parishioners devoted their energies to raising funds for a building of their own. Arthur Denny was among the trustees elected in 1872.[3] He donated a lot on Second Avenue between Spring and Seneca streets, and Captain William Renton contributed a scow of lumber from his Port Blakely mill.

In August 1873, a proud congregation assembled for dedication ceremonies, and Dr. Atkinson came from Portland to preach. Afterwards, members voted to call the Reverend Norman McLeod, a young minister from Salt Lake City who had assisted Dr. Atkinson with the service.

Sophie Frye Bass, granddaughter of Arthur and Mary Denny, attended that first Plymouth Church as a child. She

3. Arthur and Mary Denny never became members of Plymouth. Available records show he was a trustee from 1872 through 1885 and that he was active in church administration longer than any other early trustee.

later offered some recollections in her book *When Seattle Was a Village:*

> The ladies of the choir were so lovely with curls, flowers and feathers, and beruffled gowns that I decided I would be just like them when I grew up. The gentlemen were truly wonderful with their sweeping moustaches and oily locks. They displayed heavy gold watch chains over their white waistcoats embroidered with black dots.
>
> I was thrilled with my first Christmas in the little church. We children sang, "Letcher happy music on the breezes swell. Oh murry, murry Christmas time!" Over the pulpit in gold and white letters entwined with evergreens were the words, "Peace on Earth, Good Will Toward Men." The fragrance of the cedar bows will always be remembered. The tall fir tree with strings of cranberries and popcorn, and its dripping candles filled me with delight! . . . Each child was given a bag shaped like a cornucopia, made of tarletan and sewed with red yarn, which was filled with raisins, popcorn, nuts, and candy . . .
>
> My first recollection of Plymouth Church is that it was huge—really only 35 by 90 feet. Built above the street level, we had to climb a flight of steps that led from the wooden sidewalk below. In warm weather the nailheads stuck up from the wooden walk and over these we stumbled and skinned our Sunday boots. Second Avenue, which ran past the church, was ungraded and lopsided.[4]

Mrs. Bass could view the church through the wondrous eyes of a happy childhood. Seasoned members of Plymouth, however, recognized this period as difficult, not only for the church but also for the community. The wooden structure with its spired steeple stood adjacent to a grove of firs already second-growth. It had cost approximately $3,000, and a year later the debt recorded as "overwhelming" still amounted to $1,700.

Just a month before the building's dedication, the Northern Pacific Railroad announced that it had selected Tacoma instead of Seattle as its terminus on Puget Sound. This decision

4. Sophie Frye Bass, *When Seattle Was a Village* (Seattle: Lowman and Hanford, 1947), 81.

was initially interpreted as a death knell for Seattle business. The city's plight aggravated Plymouth's own financial straits, and, after just one year, Mr. McLeod resigned in 1874. Once again, the congregation was without ministerial leadership.

In the spring of 1875, the Reverend James Hall accepted Plymouth's call but lacked the spark to arouse the members. One of his sermons entitled "The Beautiful Snow" was delivered on an icy winter Sunday and lasted until long after the fire in the furnace had died out. Instead of conveying warmth and hope, Mr. Hall left his parishioners sensing only the chilly north wind and the fine snow filtering down their necks. The next Sunday when the minister preached another sermon on the same theme, one of the members suggested a postponement of services until the coming Fourth of July. Mr. Hall resigned his position after just nine months, citing his wife's ill health. Members were evidently relieved; despite the church's financial duress, they voted to give him his whole year's salary.

The turning point for fledgling Plymouth came with the arrival of the Reverend J. F. Ellis of Forest Grove, Oregon, and his wife, Mary. He assumed the pastorate in July 1876. In his quarterly report to the American Home Missionary Association the following fall, Mr. Ellis described his early impressions:

> I find here a little society apparently united and determined, disposed to give me earnest and individual support. The church is intelligent and enterprising. Its spirituality I suppose is my province to try to increase.
>
> Seattle is an intensely active little city, but the people are not church-goers. The gross and vulgar infidelity of Voltaire and Paine prevails too widely. Liquor floods nearly everything good, and religious indifference paralyzes the mass of the population. So you see that progress must be slow. There is no such thing as a spontaneous movement toward the Kingdom, but we are gaining, and that is encouraging. All agree that the moral conditions are becoming perceptibly better, and it is our purpose to put all our energy into this forward movement.

The congregation at Plymouth responded to Mr. Ellis with

The Reverend J. F. Ellis, 1876–1883

renewed energy and optimism. Mrs. George reminisced: "After he came, everything seemed different. Our debts did not seem as colossal, and the echo not impossible to overcome. People began to come to church. The Sunday School began to grow. We got a red carpet, which to us looked fine and rich. We women went down to the church and sewed it. Then the men came, carried out the pews, washed the floor, tacked down the carpet, and carried back the pews."

While the men took on the problems of heating and acoustics, the women embroidered table linens to use on sacramental occasions. Mary Ellis worked with her husband in numerous church activities, particularly on the young people's program that soon became the first Society of Christian Endeavor to be organized west of Omaha.

As church membership grew to 135, Plymouth needed more room, especially for the popular youth programs. Mr. Ellis spent his summer vacation with pick and shovel, joining other church volunteers to escavate the hillside under the church and construct a basement. The new rooms nearly doubled the building's space. They housed the Sunday school and youth programs and were the scene of numerous church socials. Supportive Plymouth households frequently managed without their dining tables so that the women of the church could stage a bazaar or chicken dinner. When they needed a dishpan or a carving knife, the women sent children scurrying down the street to the Sanderson or Waterhouse kitchen to borrow one.

Sorting Out and Extending Its Mission

Beginning with early Protestant missionaries, an anti-Catholic bias had pervaded the frontier, one from which Plymouth was not immune. Both Catholic and Protestant missionaries had ventured West to convert the Indians. In general, native people were more attracted to the black robes, silver crosses, and ritualistic Mass of the Catholics than to the comparatively unceremonious worship and threats of eternal damnation offered by the Protestants. Thus, most Protestant missionaries in the Pacific Northwest turned their attention from native Americans to new settlers, many of whom already had Protestant roots in the Midwest and New England.

In Seattle anti-Catholic sentiment ran high. In the 1870s, the Sisters of Providence opened the city's first hospital; but the Protestant majority viewed the nuns with suspicion and animosity. In a 1984 article for *The Progress*, historian Junius Rochester described Mr. Ellis' verbal attack on the order for planning to charge patients 87 cents a day for hospital services, instead of the 30 to 40 cents that the Protestant clergyman thought more in line with costs. In defense of the sisters, Father Prefontaine labeled Mr. Ellis "a falsifier of truth and a bigot of the first water" and suggested he mind his own business.

Many Protestants did seek health care from the hospital, and tensions gradually lessened. Significant ecumenical collaboration—with Plymouth as a prime instigator—was not to come about until nearly a century later.

At their 1877 annual meeting, Plymouth members adopted

a constitution, rules, and confession of faith and convenant that, even today, would be considered liberal by many churches. The statement of polity declared that the church "recognizes and maintains the absolute equality of all its members," that the church "is independent in the management of its own affairs," and that it "believes in cherishing fellowship with sister churches of our polity and order. . . ."

On the matter of the role of women, Plymouth remained in step with the times. Women of this era were elected deaconess but never deacon, trustee, clerk, or pastor. Nonetheless, women could vote and were elected to represent the church at Congregational meetings.

Because of the resourcefulness of Mr. Ellis and his parishioners, the church by the late 1870s no longer needed assistance from the American Home Missionary Association. The congregation became self-supporting in 1878 and was then able to assist other churches in the region.

By 1879, eight other Congregational churches had been organized in western Washington, and all of them were connected with the Congregational Association of Oregon and Washington. In an effort to stimulate a regional coalition for the denomination's activity, Plymouth issued a call for the first fellowship meeting in Washington, suggesting in the invitation the idea of organizing a Washington Congregational conference or association.

Delegates to the two-day session came from seven churches: Olympia, Tacoma, Port Gamble, Snohomish, White River, Fidalgo, and Seattle. Dr. Atkinson joined the group from Portland. Mrs. George recorded the Reverend Dr. Samuel Greene's later report of the outcome: "This meeting directed that invitations be issued for a permanent Association. The Oregon Association . . . stoutly opposed taking such action at that time. The Association was organized however with President A. J. Anderson of the State University (and Plymouth), as Moderator. . . . Reverend J. F. Damon preached the Associational sermon. This was the beginning of what was afterward known as the Puget Sound Association, out of which in later years came both the Northwestern and the Tacoma Associations."

In 1883 shortly after the historic conference, Mr. Ellis resigned his pastorate to accept the presidency of Pacific University in his native Forest Grove. As a leader in the denomination, he maintained active collaboration with his former parish.

Plymouth's emergence as a prominent congregation within the denomination matched Seattle's emergence as a significant city within the territory. Between 1880 and 1890, the town of some 3,500 swelled into a city of nearly 43,000. Unlike many of its neighbors on Puget Sound, Seattle was not a company town, and the mutual interaction of its diverse business enterprises stimulated rapid growth. This fortuitous situation could be credited to Arthur Denny and other like-minded pioneers who envisioned an equitable balance between management and labor. They had traded, sold, and given away parts of their claims to encourage promising new businesses.

James Colman, patriarch of a dedicated Plymouth family, is an example of a man whose prosperity created a ripple effect that promoted numerous related businesses. When Mr. Colman came to Seattle in 1876, he acquired Yesler's wharf and also took on the task of completing the so-called Seattle and Walla Walla Railroad that he eventually brought as far as the Renton coal fields (but never to Walla Walla). Access to this new source of fuel was important because the lumber industry was rapidly depleting local forests. In addition to opening up the coal-mining industry, Mr. Colman's railroad made Seattle the channel for farming and logging trade with the hinterlands.

For Plymouth the 1880s were likewise years of major growth and transition as the church began to take a more active role in the community. In tune with the mood of the city, the Reverend Frank Taylor arrived in 1884 to become an ardent promoter of Seattle and Plymouth. His magnetism is said to have drawn brothers Edward and Anson Burwell to Seattle and to have prompted Dr. Edward C. Kilbourne to forsake his Episcopalian roots in favor of Congregationalism. These three men, along with other young community activists, entered into all phases of church work and extended their mission into a lifetime of involvement in civic concerns.

Mr. Taylor's ministry at Plymouth was meteoric, ending abruptly after just six months when he accidently shot and

The Reverend Frank Taylor, 1884

killed himself while hunting on Squak Slough (now Issaquah). In her book, Mrs. Rayner says: "The young people, who had adored him, stripped the summer gardens of flowers to decorate the church for his funeral, and above the pulpit alcove where he had stood so short a time before they placed the floral motto—'I go, do ye my work.' In the spirit of that text they resolved to carry on."

While at Oberlin, the Burwell brothers had known the Reverend Henry L. Bates. Acting on their recommendation, members called the young minister to his first pastorate. He arrived in the fall of 1884 with his wife, Cora. Mr. Bates was well suited to the rapidly expanding community and congregation. He joined Mr. Colman's sons Laurence and George and C. E. "Scotty" Bowman in a popular men's quartet. The ensemble reconvened frequently in later years whenever Mr. Bates returned to Seattle to visit his former parish.

During this period, Colman family members established

The Reverend Henry L. Bates, 1884–1889

the tradition of taking various church groups on eagerly awaited outings and camping trips aboard their yacht "Latona." Among the most popular destinations were the undeveloped, forest-lined beaches of West Seattle. During one of the premiere outings to Orcas Island, the young people gave a concert and on their way home spent the night at the newly established Congregational Academy in Coupeville to which Plymouth had contributed funds.

Seattle rode the youthful tide of optimism into the early 1880s and then found itself struggling against the undertow of the economic panic of 1883 that dragged the nation into a deep depression. Because of a diverse and healthy economic base, Seattle was better equipped than most of its Puget Sound neighbors to weather the storm. As a result, desperate young men, women, and entire families were coming to the city in hopes of finding work. In this period predating a government social-welfare system, destitute people foraged for food, often

The 1886 wedding of Leilla Shorey (daughter of Oliver and Mary) and Dr. Edward C. Kilbourne was the first between two Plymouth young people. The groom described the church as a bower of flowers and said: "Everybody came whether invited or not. I was one of those who did not receive an invitation, but I was there, dressed in a Prince Albert and white tie. I stood beside the bride, the better to show off her beautiful cream-white lace dress."

attempting to subsist on a diet of clams and salmon. Plymouth was among supporters of the various city missions that sought to ameliorate the situation.

The Apple Orchard Convention

Perhaps a new awareness of desperate women and families is what drew Plymouth's attention to the squalid part of town where poor and transient people lived. For years propertied churchgoers had decried the thriving dens of iniquity in what was known as "the Tenderloin" south of Mill Street (now Yesler Way). There saloons, bawdyhouses, gambling dens, and distilleries operated openly.

Prior to the 1880s, Seattle's more fortunate citizens who lived on the hill overlooking Elliott Bay did little to clean up the Tenderloin. For the most part they averted their gaze, concentrating instead on building their churches, schools, and businesses. Despite this disdain for the vice district, the city readily accepted the considerable tax revenues generated by prosperous brothel owners and saloonkeepers.

Acts of protest did, however, occur. In 1879, an anonymous zealot set fire to the Illahee, a notorious "squaw brothel," so-called because some of the prostitutes there were native American. With all of the drama of the legendary Wild West, a mob of vigilantes in 1881 stormed the court and jail to vindicate the separate shootings of a policeman and grocery clerk. Overpowering the guards, the mob dragged out three prisoners awaiting trial for the offenses and lynched them from the nearest trees.

Protestant churches, the Good Templars, and the Women's Christian Temperance Union were among organizations that had long wanted to stamp out vice. Until the 1880s, however, they did more talking than acting. Vice-related violence finally drew together idealistic reformers. Linking the issue of women's suffrage with temperance, proponents of law and order in 1883 successfully lobbied the Territorial Legislature to grant women the right to vote. This move was calculated to swing the balance of power to the side of virtue and, at least temporarily, it had the desired result.

Plymouth Church was the site of the initial meeting of Seattle reformers who in 1884 organized the Law and Order League and who from the start counted on the support of newly enfranchised women. The League's purpose was to pressure city officials and police to enforce existing laws and to enact new ones to purge the Tenderloin. Called the Apple Orchard Convention because the first meeting was outdoors under Plymouth's neighboring trees, the session produced a slate of candidates who handily won in the next city and county elections.

Sin in Seattle was dealt a stunning blow. Brothels and saloons were suddenly closed. Sunday blue laws were enforced, and perpetrators of vice were prosecuted. Proper townsfolk proudly congratulated themselves.

In a 1985 article for *The Weekly*, historian David M. Buerge aptly put Seattle's first reform movement into perspective: "In their zeal, the Apple Orchardists revealed themselves as the forerunners of the Populists and Progressives of later decades. Like others in cities across the country, they had begun to grapple with the immense problems spawned by industrialization and urbanization, and applied the idealism of the gospels to heal the ills of society. By interpreting the gospel message less as a call for personal repentance, they authored what has since become known as the Social Gospel movement in American Protestantism."

Not surprisingly, Seattle's clean sweep of the vice district was short-lived. As the recession plummeted to new depths, city coffers and legitimate businesses felt the squeeze. On their days off loggers and miners took their paychecks to less-snobbish communities where they could squander the money at will. As a result, Seattle's economy slumped.

Within a year the Apple Orchardists were voted out of office, and the city's saloons and brothels were back in business. Responding to pressure primarily from drinking men, the Territorial Supreme Court in 1887 ruled the women's vote unconstitutional. The pendulum of power had swung back and would continue to elude reformers until 1910 when Washington women finally reclaimed the franchise.

Anti-Chinese Riots

Growing numbers of Chinese added to the population influx

of the eighties. After fulfilling their contracts to lay track for the transcontinental railroad, the Chinese established homes in Pacific Coast cities. Unlike most other immigrant groups, Chinese men had not assimilated into the predominantly white community. As a consequence, they became the target of racist ridicule and suspicion.

To curb the Chinese immigrants' impact on the labor market and on Western society, Congress in 1882 passed the unprecedented Chinese Restriction Act. It prohibited further immigration and denied permanent residence to Chinese already here who were not citizens. Newly settled bachelors could not legally send home for their brides, wives, or families. In the resulting male-dominated "Chinatowns," opium, gambling, and prostitution were said to have supplanted family life.

Organized by Chinese merchants, men imported to make up work gangs for the railroads now began to compete with white laborers for jobs. The Wa Chong Company ran daily ads in the *Seattle Post-Intelligencer* for cheap labor. Uncomplaining, the "johns" would work for less than other men at the most hazardous and menial jobs. Striking miners from Newcastle and others of the local unemployed grew restive. They were influenced by anti-Chinese agitators from the Knights of Labor who saw Chinese men working while white men sat idle.

In 1885, the massacre of Chinese in Rock Springs, Wyoming, triggered riots and violence throughout the West. Vigilantes fired on Chinese hop pickers in Squak Valley, killing three. Fearing similar reprisals, Territorial Governor Watson Squire (who was in Seattle at the time) declared martial law, and notices were immediately sent to the churches.

Dr. Kilbourne later recalled what happened: " 'The Agitators,' we called them, vented their spite on the Chinese and tried to drive them out of Seattle. Trouble was anticipated. The Home Guard was organized, composed of merchants, lawyers, judges, preachers, and others. Mr. Bates, our pastor, joined the Home Guard. I was a member of the Militia Company. One Sunday at six in the morning, the Agitators and the teamsters, with their wagons, herded the Chinese with such

Harper's Weekly depicted members of the Home Guard protecting Chinese from an angry mob. Protectors included Plymouth men and their minister.

of their belongings as they could quickly pick up, down to the Ocean dock between Washington and Main Street."

While bells rang out from the Methodist Church and the university, Mr. Bates read the governor's proclamation and then marched down from the pulpit, his rifle in hand. Followed by several other men in the congregation, he hurried to the Armory just across the street. There the men of Plymouth joined forces with other defenders of law and order to quell the riot.

Assuming that Mr. Bates and his militant parishioners were motivated by a sense of racial justice would be incorrect. In the 1880s, some Plymouth members most likely took advantage of the cheap labor by employing Chinese servants or relying on Chinese businesses to do their laundry. At a time when Americans were out of work, citizens took up arms in defense of law and order; simultaneously, they condemned the illegal alien, which many Chinese were thought to be.

People began to lose their sense of perspective. Before long, even the Chinese who had immigrated legally came to be viewed as part of the "yellow peril" and were ostracized on the basis of race. Proper members of the city's newly established women's organizations openly favored their extradition.

Everett Smith arrived in Seattle in 1885 where he became a member of Plymouth and later a judge. In his initial correspondence with his finance, Mary Dibble, he made the following observations about the city's Indians and Chinese: "Hundreds of Indians are on and about the streets of this cosmopolitan town now, stopping in the city to spend the money earned in the hop fields. One hop grower has employed a thousand for nearly a month picking a few miles out of the city. The harbor swarms with their canoes. They are harmless, filthy creatures. Worse than these are the 800 Chinese in the city."

He fails to explain why the Chinese were worse but goes on to express the motivation of law-abiding citizens—among them the people of Plymouth. It was to uphold law and order and to avoid bloodshed. In Mr. Smith's words, "The anti-Chinese demonstrations of the rougher elements have been so frequent and threatening of late that the law abiding citizens last night held a semi-secret meeting and organized regular companies to turn out in case of disturbance of the peace. About 800 were sworn in—yours truly among the number—as deputy sheriffs to act if needed."

Although citizens organized to protect the Chinese and their property from the angry mob, few voiced any regret when in January of 1886 most of Seattle's Chinese voluntarily boarded steamers bound for San Francisco. Their passage had been raised by white people who wanted them to leave. To Seattle's credit, defenders of law and order did protect the Chinese from the slaughter they experienced at the hands of bloodthirsty mobs in other communities. A fall 1899 *Plym-*

outh Church Herald welcomed back Len Jong, "our only Chinese member and personal friend" upon his return from a two-year visit to his homeland. Unlike the anonymous "yellow horde," he had been a friend.

A 'Mother' Church

As more and more people came to Seattle, its residential districts began to spread beyond the downtown area. In response, Plymouth now assumed the role of a "mother" church, helping establish Congregational parishes in outlying neighborhoods.

David and Louisa Boren Denny had staked their original claim to the north of the city in the area between Lake Union and Elliott Bay. In 1887, they offered to give the church a lot in the "Park Addition" bordering on the five-acre tract (later named Denny Park) that they had already donated to the city. The new congregation was named Taylor Memorial in honor of Plymouth's ill-fated former pastor and was the first of what would become a large family of neighborhood "daughter" churches.

On several occasions Plymouth members planted the roots of a new church by starting what was then called a "Sunday school." Pilgrim Chapel was one. It was established at approximately the same time as Taylor Memorial. In both cases, laymen from Plymouth conducted the initial Sunday afternoon services.

Everett Smith and "the Colman and Burwell boys" devoted considerable time and effort to organizing Pilgrim. In a March 1887 letter to Mary Dibble, Mr. Smith described some of his activities: "(After supper) I mounted the Colman cayuse and rode to Pilgrim Chapel. I found things about as I expected. The carpenter at work had left the room in confusion, the floor littered with shavings and the seats tumbled together. I worked an hour with the broom and then had things in good shape. Only one week more of Pilgrim Chapel efforts. All the work will be completed during this week and next week some evening we shall have an 'opening.' On that occasion I shall act the role of lecturer and give a stereopticon show for a half hour. The choir will help with songs."

A year later he wrote a letter pondering the future of Pilgrim Chapel because he would have to be away from Seattle during the summer. He said: "I believe it will be best for the school and for me to dissolve after June. The Lord has some worker in the city who will take my place and more than fill it. I shall be ready at another time to take up Sunday school work again, but two years in one capacity is enough for a while. . . . Today I went to Chapel to services, but our minister Mr. Dawson did not appear. He lives nearly a mile away and I suppose the day was too stormy for him. The wind has blown nearly a hurricane all day. Once in a long time we have such windstorms, but they are rare."

True to his resolve, two years after completing his work at Pilgrim, Mr. Smith in 1890 secured a lot, along with one-fourth of the needed money to enable Plymouth to establish a Sunday school on Yesler Avenue. He then arranged purchase of a building on Joy Street to which Plymouth members contributed $400 plus their old pump organ for yet another Sunday school.

Also in 1890, Plymouth voted to accept the proposition of the Methodist Protestants who wished to sell their Sunday school on Jackson Street for $2,000 and have Plymouth's young people take charge. While organizing Sunday schools, Plymouth also provided financial and other assistance to additional neighborhood churches, among them the fledgling Fremont congregation.

A New Downtown—A New Plymouth

The time of rapid expansion for Seattle's Congregational denomination was also a time of upheaval and resurgence for the city, sparked by a catastrophe. On June 6, 1889, a fire broke out in a First Avenue woodworking shop and quickly spread to engulf 58 blocks of the downtown business area. As city leaders surveyed the smoldering remains of wooden buildings, they estimated the loss to be nearly $10 million.

The Reverend George A. Tewksbury, 1889–1891

The previous January, Mr. Bates had resigned from Plymouth to become a teacher. His replacement, the Reverend George A. Tewksbury, arrived in Seattle with his wife, Virginia Lee, just after the fire to witness an almost surrealistic wasteland. Plymouth's wood-frame building had been spared; but almost everything to its south and west was a mass of charred debris.

In retrospect, the conflagration may have been serendipitous. Like the mythological phoenix, a modern city soon rose from the ashes, this time constructed of stone and brick. Local businesses prospered, especially the building trades, and property values skyrocketed.

Because of a significant increase in membership, Plymouth found its little pioneer building no longer adequate. Also, if the church were to continue to attract new members, it needed to keep pace with the contemporary look of its commercial neighbors.

Plymouth's spire still stands in the background (center left) in this photo by John P. Soule taken after the June 6, 1889, Great Seattle Fire. Buildings within a half block of the church were destroyed. National Guardsmen stationed at the intersection of First Avenue and Columbia Street take seriously their job of thwarting would-be looters. (Courtesy University of Washington Photography Collection)

In July the congregation voted to sell its 20-year-old building on Second Avenue and to erect a new structure. According to Dr. Kilbourne's account, members felt that "there should be no swapping of horses in the middle of the stream;" so they reelected him and his fellow trustees to an unprecedented second term. Having abandoned dentistry for a more lucrative real-estate business, Dr. Kilbourne negotiated the sale of the old property for $32,000 and secured an option on two lots at Third Avenue and University Street.

Before leaving the old building, Plymouth invited 25 other churches to send delegates to Mr. Tewksbury's formal installation, the first service of its kind in Washington. Mrs. Rayner wrote that he adhered to the ceremonious New England tradition and "gave a most thorough and explicit statement of Christian experience and doctrinal belief," whereupon he was accepted by the delegates. Plymouth was deeply honored when the Reverend Cushing Eells delivered the installation sermon. He was a founder of Whitman College in Walla Walla and one of the American Board's first missionaries in the Spokane area, settling there in 1839.

While the congregation raised funds for a new building and simultaneously supported satellite Sunday schools, members worshipped in a temporary structure that was hastily erected on the new property. The coffers swelled, as did the membership, and Plymouth kept pace with the ubiquitous construction and development that typified the reemerging city.

The product of a staid New England upbringing, Mr. Tewksbury found the frenetic pace of church activities and informality of the temporary building almost intolerable. In March of 1891, he deemed it "wise and best to resign the pastoral connection," hoping that in due time the congregation "may secure another man, thoroughly adapted in all ways to the work."

Unwittingly, Mr. Tewksbury had zeroed in on a characteristic that was to typify Plymouth. He recognized a congregation unfettered by nostalgia and ready to adapt its thinking, program, and facility to the changing needs of the downtown community.

2
The Boom Years 1890–1910

The years between 1891 and 1910 marked Seattle's rapid transition from a frontier outpost to the premiere city of the Pacific Northwest. They also marked the emergence of Plymouth as a church firmly planted in its community, one that during this period would strengthen its ability to nurture members and put into practice a social gospel.

The healthy, broad-based business climate attracted new enterprise, and the arrival of the transcontinental railway bolstered commerce. Following the economic panic of 1893 that rocked the nation, rich and poor swarmed to Seattle. Those having money and skills came with optimism; those with neither came out of desperation, hoping for at least a chance to survive. Between 1890 and 1900, the population nearly doubled from some 43,000 to more than 80,600, and in the following decade it tripled, reaching just over 237,000.

Seattle of the gay and not-so-gay nineties provided an intriguing challenge for urban planners who were beginning to conceptualize elaborate schemes for sluicing down the city's precipitous hills and reclaiming muddy tide flats with the residue. While Pioneer Square developed as the nucleus of the business district, the retail core was near the site of Plymouth's first building. Frederick & Nelson, the Bon Marché, and Munro were among the stores making their debuts. Nestled between the business and retail districts was the center of downtown where Arthur and Mary Denny's cow grazed contentedly in her pasture at First Avenue and University Street. Overlooking the Denny homestead was the 10-acre University Tract. When the University of Washington moved classes to its new North End campus in 1898, the original buildings downtown met the need for student dormitories.

Seattle's First Large Brick Church

In the summer of 1891, members of Plymouth and their new pastor, the Reverend Dr. Wallace Nutting, watched with pride and eager anticipation as their stately red-brick edifice rose with a lofty spire and two smaller towers. It stood at the corner of Third Avenue and University Street, a serene location between the University Tract and the Denny homestead.

Work proceeded quickly. In October the congregation was able to move from temporary quarters at the Armory into the Sunday school rooms on the lower floor of the church. In January 1892, a new publication, the *Plymouth Church Herald,* proudly announced the building's completion: "We lack only the organ and pews. Inasmuch as the floor of the auditorium slopes, it will not be comfortable to attempt seating it with chairs. We must wait another month."

But in booming Seattle, patience was not a popular virtue. Another month was too long for the ever-resourceful Dr. Kilbourne, who devised a plan to adapt the chairs to the sloping floor by shortening their back legs. For many years thereafter, Plymouth members and their guests were occasionally reminded of this ingenious innovation when at large church dinners they found themselves seated on strangely low, tipped-back chairs.

Within a short time the new sanctuary was complete. Oak pews, arranged in semicircular, amphitheater fashion, could seat 800 people. Behind the pulpit rose the arched choir alcove and the great pipe organ, a gift of the women of the church. One of the popular attractions was church music, enhanced by the auditorium's excellent acoustics. With L. A. Darling as organist and choirmaster, the 12-member choir drew some of the city's best talent.

Dr. Nutting had a demanding schedule. He had no paid staff and relied solely on volunteers for support. On Sunday morning the congregation filled the sanctuary; children, their parents, and their grandparents worshiped together from many family pews. Bible school followed at 12:30 P.M., after which volunteers went to the three branch Sunday schools for mid-afternoon programs and services. The Young People's Society of Christian Endeavor met at 6:45 P.M., and members

The Reverend Dr. Wallace Nutting, 1891–1895

and their guests returned en masse for an evening service with sermon and choir.

Weekdays at the church were also lively with a variety of regularly scheduled activities, including receptions at the parsonage on Tuesdays, evening discussions of the Columbian Chautauqua Literary and Scientific Circle on Wednesdays, and the almost-imperative evening prayer meetings on Thursdays. Augusta Burwell characterized the early church as the nucleus of spiritual as well as social and cultural life for most of its members: "We were very closely bonded, because we knew each other so well."

One of the minister's many obligations was to be the official church visitor. His wife, Mariet Griswold Nutting, often accompanied him. A summer 1892 issue of the *Herald* notes that, during his first year in the new church, Dr. Nutting "has made a thousand calls, but owing to the fact that many of these

The church at Third Avenue and University Street was large—but not large enough to seat everyone who came to this last service before Plymouth vacated

were upon new families, some of the members of long standing have not been called upon.''

Old and new members and a host of guests gravitated to Seattle's first modern, brick church. Some came by horse and buggy from newly developed outlying areas, and others still lived within easy walking distance. Within a year membership had doubled. By 1893, the congregation filled the 800-seat sanctuary, leaving latecomers out of luck.

In their new building Dr. Nutting and the trustees promoted plans for expansion almost from the beginning. In the spring of 1893, trustees recommended enlarging the church to give seating for 1,200, with an additional 250 seats to be gained by building a Sunday school room on the vacant lot north of the church and connecting the two sections with

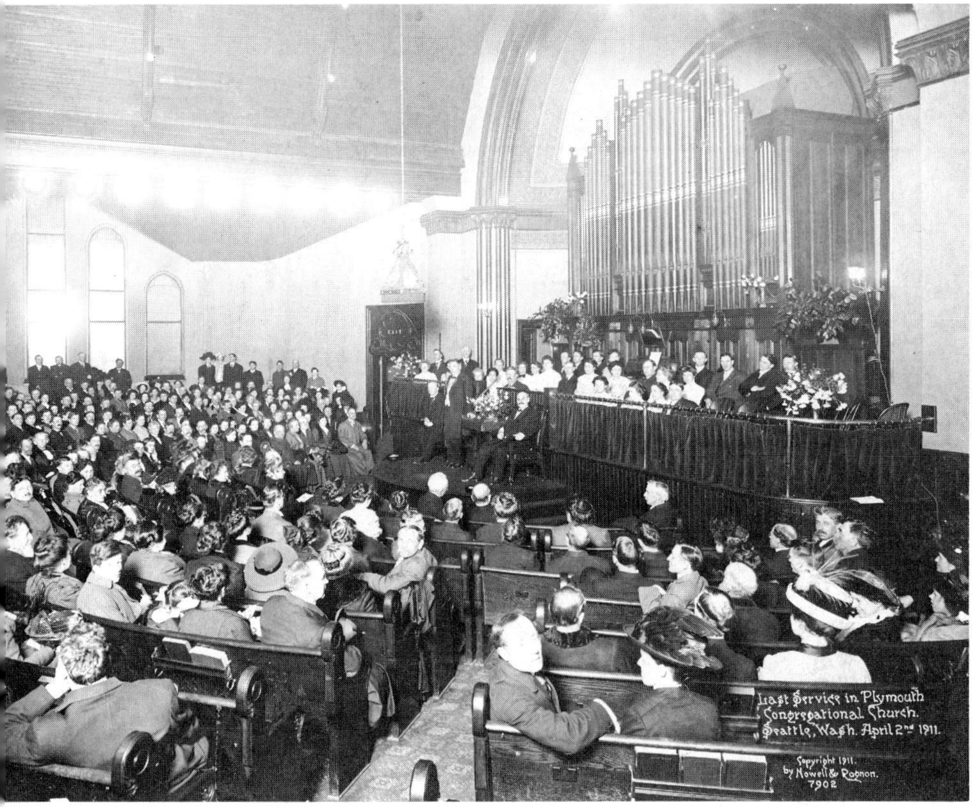

the building. Note that many of the women are holding their stylish hats on their knees in consideration of parishioners seated behind them.

sliding doors. When the women were still raising funds to retire the debt on the $6,000 organ and when other debts were still owing, the thought of securing additional amounts for expansion must have been discouraging. In any case the fervor seems to have yielded to the budget, and the church remained as it was originally built.

An uncompromising opponent of any hint of vice, Dr. Nutting used his pulpit to promote what he called "heroic remedies." Members of the congregation who strayed from the straight and narrow could expect to be publicly chastened. On one occasion a group of members arranged a raffle or some such "petty gambling game" without Dr. Nutting's knowledge. He later wrote, "Instead of working quietly to change this, I referred in severe terms from the platform to the pernicious practice by which a church set the pace for all other associations . . . in contenancing gambling of any sort."[1] The husband of one of the women involved told Dr. Nutting that, by his action, the pastor had just lost his influence in the church and the city. Attendance at Plymouth, however, continued to increase.

Another time Dr. Nutting came out strongly against church people's renting out their property for "liquor places." He wrote, "A deacon, a dear friend, withdrew from the church because he was an offender in this respect." In a margin note Dr. Kilbourne later penciled in the name Sanderson—probably John Sanderson, one of Plymouth's six founding members.

Despite the fact that it pained him to humiliate his friends and parishioners, Dr. Nutting felt that the credibility of the church was at stake and that the city would believe in a church that stood behind its principles. He was highly esteemed, as evidenced by his honorary doctorate from Whitman College awarded in 1893 and Plymouth's invitation to return as summer supply pastor in 1930. By that time he had gained international recognition for his photography and his "States Beautiful" books about early-American life.

After four years at Plymouth during which the congregation had nearly tripled, Dr. Nutting resigned in early 1895 to return to a less-tumultuous New England parish. His successor, the Reverend Dr. W. H. G. Temple, was a man of boundless energy who would remain at the church's helm for 10 years, a heretofore unprecedented length of service. A feisty native of Nova Scotia, Dr. Temple was well suited to the frenetic pace that awaited him when he and his wife, Julia, arrived in Seattle in the summer of 1895.

The local press was drawn to Plymouth's colorful new minister who maintained that "no man had a right to preach who didn't wilt a collar during a sermon."[2] Within a few weeks of his arrival, *The Seattle Times* was printing the Sunday

1. Wallace Nutting, *Wallace Nutting's Biography* (Framingham, MA: Old America Company, 1936), 29–30.

2. Alice E. Rayner, *The Path We Came By: A History of Plymouth Congregational Church* (Seattle, 1937), 45.

The Reverend Dr. W. H. G. Temple, 1895–1905

evening sermons, and the *Seattle Post-Intelligencer* published the Sunday morning message. In the spring of 1896, Dr. Temple expressed in the *Herald* his delight: "The human voice can reach but few after all, but the cylinders of the press can multiply audiences indefinitely, and so spread the Gospel widely among the homes of the people."

With the press as a vehicle for attracting newcomers to religion and to Plymouth, he sometimes oriented his sermons to specific professional groups, among them servicemen, schoolteachers, and attorneys. On one occasion he invited the whole Seattle legal fraternity to come to Plymouth for his Sunday sermon on law and the Bible. When Seattle's major newspapers quit publishing sermons, *The Seattle Times* donated typesetting so that the *Herald* could be expanded to include a "Sermon for Shut-ins."

The previously dignified *Herald* was transformed by the

THE CRESCENT

DRY GOODS, NOTIONS AND FURNISHINGS

New Store, New Goods, and Right Prices 1327 First Avenue

UMBRELLAS You'll save 25 per cent of your money by buying your umbrellas of us.

And you'll get the best makes, we repair any that goes wrong FREE

SHAMEK'S 1221 FIRST AVENUE, Near Postoffice

WANTED: Young men, of good address, to travel and represent our company. Call and talk with us. **CHOICE PORTRAIT CO.**

217-19-21 First Avenue South and Jackson Street, Seattle, Wash.

minister's no-nonsense style. In the pages of the spring 1897 issue, Dr. Temple exhorted all to "intense activity in the cause of Christ" and admonished church members to adopt the uncompromising motto, "I will let nothing but sickness or death prevent me from being at my church both morning and evening every Sunday in the year." A stickler for punctuality and reliability, Dr. Temple made a point of listing in the *Herald* the Sunday school classes with perfect attendance. Those with the best records warranted banners and stars.

Much to the chagrin of some of the parishioners, the thrifty new pastor in 1895 made the *Herald* self-supporting by selling full-page advertising. In the ads Drs. C. A. Gay and Baker boasted that they could fill and extract teeth without pain and without using chloroform or cocaine. Other ads promoted osteopathy "guaranteed to cure 60% of incurable cases"; Greyhound motor-coach runs to Everett; Adams Cash Grocer with fresh Iowa creamery butter; steamer runs to the Klondike; and Madame Elliot's palmistry.

Censorship was apparently not an issue for Dr. Temple. He zealously supported his patrons with personal endorsements such as: "Who can repeat with eyes shut the names of our advertisers? You ought to have them by heart, so when you pass their place of business and want anything in their line you can say—'They advertise in the *Herald*; I guess I'll buy my goods there.' " Many members of Plymouth must have heaved a sigh of relief when in 1902 the congregation voted to finance the paper by voluntary subscription so that it could be "wholly divested of the commercial idea."

Politically, Dr. Temple used the pulpit to urge his congregation and his extended audience to support Plymouth's Judge W. D. Wood in his bid to become mayor of Seattle. Campaigning in 1895 on a reform ticket, Judge Wood trumpeted the ecumenically supported causes of a new city charter and the closure of saloons on Sundays. While admonishing the men of Plymouth not to miss their Thursday evening prayer meeting, Dr. Temple also gave them a way out. During the campaign, he wrote in the *Herald:* "If the deacons or other voters can do anything at caucuses, primaries, or conventions for pure municipal government, they are hereby commended. When the pastor can be of service, let him know, and he will appoint a deacon to lead the meeting, and leave the women to pray for us men, while we do our religious duty toward our city. The first duty is to register."

When Judge Wood won the election, Dr. Temple rejoiced, writing in the *Herald,* "What comfort it is to have a praying man our presiding civic officer!" Two years later, however, vice again triumphed over virtue. Dr. Temple described newly elected Mayor T. J. Humes as "a man defiant of the laws."

Among the new members who joined Plymouth during Mayor Wood's term of office were Alden J. and Rose A. Blethen, owners of *The Seattle Times,* and Professor Henry and Bertha Landes. Mrs. Landes could not have foreseen at the time that she would one day be elected Seattle's mayor. After all, women would have to wait until 1910 to be able to vote.

Sunday School and Youth Programs

By 1890, Seattle boasted 12 public schools, including one high school. Plymouth was reaching out to bring the Sunday school experience to as many children and youth as possible. The devoted volunteer staff maintained programs at the downtown church as well as at Pilgrim Chapel, Joy Street, and Jackson Street. As children became involved in Sunday school, their parents often followed to become active members of the church.

Plymouth continued its long-standing tradition of supporting public education and schoolteachers. At the time, women had to remain single or lose their teaching jobs. In 1882, Anson and Gertrude Burwell established the custom of inviting all of the new teachers in the city's schools to spend a September Saturday at their summer home on Bainbridge Island. Many of them joined the church, prompting Mr. Burwell to organize a class especially for single young women, most of whom were teachers.

By the turn of the century this "normal class" had grown so popular that members created the Anson Burwell Class Association. It convened for monthly dinner meetings until 1955 when the membership decided to move to a less-formal structure. At these meetings the women had devotions, planned fund-raising events, dispersed donations to foreign missions, organized services for the needy in their own community, and enjoyed presentations by guest speakers. In conjunction with the founding of this association, Plymouth instituted the popular 10-cent church suppers on Thursdays for schoolteachers who were required to stay downtown that evening for teachers' meetings.

In the spring of 1903, the average attendance in the Sunday school was 300 to 400, too low for Sunday School Superintendent Judge Wood. He declared that he wanted to boost the school to a thousand members. Rallying to the challenge, trustees and the minister concluded that the time had finally come for Plymouth to hire a pastoral assistant who would also be associate superintendent of the Sunday school.

In its early years, Plymouth's Sunday school was the product of the frontier spirit—the "can-do" inventiveness that compelled everyone to do what had to be done as best they could. More recently, the Christian Endeavor movement had added to the fervor, with adults' volunteering to assume even greater responsibilities. Plymouth had, indeed, been fortunate in having high-caliber volunteers who were deeply committed to youth work and the Sunday school.

These volunteers, however, recognized their limitations. They were eager for guidance from a theologically schooled in-

Plymouth's Carrie Shumway taught at Central School and was also a vocal proponent for public education in early Seattle. (Courtesy Seattle Public Schools Archives)

dividual who could bring needed structure and foundation to the religious training program. As they began their search for the first Sunday school director, trustees vowed to find someone with the same youthful, enthusiastic spirit that had always characterized Plymouth volunteers. At all costs they determined to reject "old fogyism." Affectionately nicknamed "Sunny Jim," James Lynch met all of their requirements. His coming to the Sunday school in 1903 marked the beginning of a new era of programmed religious instruction.

Mr. Lynch immediately teamed with Judge Wood, pitting the Reds against the Blues in a rollicking recruitment contest

On Christian Endeavor Day in February of 1901, the Plymouth chancel is festooned with flags and garlands to memorialize Britian's Queen Victoria who had died the month before.

to triple Sunday school enrollment. With programs and activities for all age groups, anyone was fair game. New members shared the excitement, proudly sporting their "Plymouth 1 of 1,000" buttons. On the last Sunday of the year, the goal of 1,000 members was reached with the Blues nosing out the Reds by just five recruits.

Dr. Temple embraced the Christian Endeavor movement that was rapidly gaining both national and international momentum. He edited the *Washington Endeavorer* and expanded the program at Plymouth. It grew to include senior, intermediate, and junior societies, all of which met on Sunday evenings for fellowship and discussion. Among its activities the Junior Society funded one of the city's first drinking fountains, directly in front of the church. The Intermediate Society assumed long-term responsibility for decorating the pulpit. The young people also arranged to have the church's first telephone installed.

Like the Christian Endeavor societies, Sunday school classes also contributed to the church and community. Mrs. A. B. Stewart's class called the "Willing Workers" organized a fruit and flower mission to bring cheer to the sick, and Dr. Kilbourne's class of young women purchased an upright piano for the lecture room of the church.

Adult Fellowship

Idleness seems to have been intolerable for Dr. Temple. In addition to youth programs, he initiated numerous fellowship organizations for groups of all ages and interests. Among these were the Brotherhood of Andrew and Philip, the Young Women's League, the Men's Club, and the Ladies' Aid Society.

The first president of the Plymouth Men's Club was James Moore, the city's leading real-estate developer. Among numerous other projects, he built Seattle's first elegant residential hotel, the Lincoln, at Fourth Avenue and Madison Street. Julia Temple and her husband lived at the Lincoln where they graciously entertained friends from the nearby, overcrowded church. James and Bessie Moore also lived there; as president of the Ladies' Aid Society, she hosted meetings in her commodious apartment and used the hotel lobby for elaborately staged bazaars.

The newly organized Men's Club also enjoyed the hotel's facilities where members sometimes had their monthly dinners. The women faithfully prepared and served these dinners, and once a year on "Ladies' Night," the men reciprocated by hosting the women. While appreciating the women's work, members of the Men's Club nonetheless supported Judge Everett Smith in his long-term campaign against stylish, wide-brimmed, flower-bedecked hats. Appeals such as the following frequently appeared in 1907 issues of the *Herald:* "Will the ladies kindly remove their hats, unless they are perfectly sure no one behind them is inconvenienced."

The George Colman Boys' Club

Along with their church activities, some Plymouth people were taking a lead in nonsectarian service organizations. Dr. Kilbourne was on the board of the YMCA, a position that he would actively maintain for most of his long life. During her years at Plymouth, Caroline Sanderson carried forth her commitments as a founding member of the Ladies' Relief Society (now Seattle Children's Home), the Ladies' Library Association (forerunner of the Seattle Public Library), and the Seattle Red Cross. Emma Wallingford Wood, Mary Shorey, and several others devoted their energies to the Women's Christian Temperance Union and also helped found the Seattle YWCA. That organization's initial purpose was to thwart the "white slavers" in Seattle's red-light district by providing needed resources for destitute young women.

Similarly, George Colman's heart went out to the local Artful Dodgers and Oliver Twists who, along with fishermen, dock workers, and the down and out, made their homes in the waterfront shacks west of First Avenue. Some of the boys earned a pittance by selling newspapers and running errands, and others belonged to the notorious Bell Town Gang or the Seventh Street Devils.

Mr. Colman routinely walked the streets, making friends with the boys who hawked the morning news. In 1899, he began to invite those who were idle to join his afternoon Sunday school class that met in the alluring tower room of the church. With a combination of scripture, hymns, and inspirational talks tailored to the boys' interests, Mr. Colman attracted a steadily increasing and devoted following. Other parishioners (some of whom were frightened at first) soon joined in helping. As the class rapidly expanded, its activities were moved into the larger Sunday school rooms where, according to Mrs. Rayner, the boys "made themselves very much at home, to the dismay and shock of the church ladies, who considered them impossible young savages." With growing enthusiasm for the work, even the most recalcitrant among Plymouth's members became supportive of this effort.

By the end of 1899, more than 50 of the ragged lads were enrolled in the afternoon class. From the beginning Mr.

Edith Sanderson (later Mrs. W. N. Redfield) followed in the footsteps of her mother, Caroline Sanderson, by contributing notably to Plymouth's Sunday school and to voluntary organizations in the community.

Colman planned programs and special events open to boys with regular Sunday school attendance records. In an effort to provide them with a wholesome outlet during the week, he organized the Plymouth Boys' Club. Members at first met biweekly for an evening of games, singing, and refreshments. Older boys attended the Plymouth Boys' School, a Friday evening manual-training class that originated in the church kitchen where volunteer instructors brought tools and lumber from home.

When an addition to the building was completed in 1908, the Boys' Club and other youth groups had their own spacious quarters. To expand the popular manual-training program, Mr. Colman contributed a shop complete with all kinds of hand and power tools. By this time regular membership had increased to nearly 200 boys. The new church occupied in 1912 would include two manual-training shops in support of the program, as well as a modern gymnasium with locker room and showers.

Nurturing good character and helping underprivileged boys become upstanding citizens were always the goals of the Boys' Club; but over time some of the original procedures changed. Mr. Colman and the other volunteers at first felt that physical sports should be downplayed in favor of quieter activities that would deter too much excitability. Among Plymouth members, however, were many who enjoyed and appreciated athletics. Perhaps the precedent set by regional Congregational college teams brought about the leadership's change of heart. A fall 1901 issue of the *Herald* notes: "Significant! Whitman beat the University of Washington at football lately; and now Puget Sound Academy has beaten the U of W Preps. Anyone would think Congregationalism had considerable kicking ability!"

Within a short time the value of sports was widely acknowledged at Plymouth, and the YMCA pitched in to direct an ambitious physical-education and recreation program. When the church opened its new building in 1912, boys aged 8 to 18 used its gymnasium six days a week. Graded activities there included ping-pong, badminton, boxing, and basketball. Interest in sports continued over the years; in the 1930s, the Boys' Club boasted seven basketball teams in the city league.

Free membership in the YMCA was among incentives for the boys to maintain near-perfect records of Sunday school attendance. Among eagerly anticipated special events were periodic banquets, informal bean feeds, and the annual Christmas dinner, for which George Colman's mother, Agnes, always contributed roast turkey with all the trimmings. At the end of the school year, the boys and their Sunday school teachers boarded the Colman yacht "Osprey" for their annual trip to Blake Island with Laurence Colman as captain, George as fireman, and their father, James, as engineer.

Among other trips, the boys enjoyed outings to Snoqualmie, English Camp, Doe Bay, and the San Juan Islands. The first year of the summer camp on Blake Island is unre-

Spirited games of basketball in the Plymouth gymnasium were a favorite way for Boys' Club members to learn team play and cement friendships.

corded; but the free week of outdoor work and play soon became the most compelling inducement for attending Sunday school. In later years the boys had their camp on Colman property at Horsehead Bay on Hood Canal.

While many Plymouth men and women were associated with the Boys' Club, Mr. Colman was undeniably the driving and sustaining force. As a tribute, members changed the name to the George Colman Boys' Club. In the Rayner history, Mary Dowling Ritchie recorded that Mr. Colman enjoyed baseball, tennis, and water sports, all features of the outings sponsored by his family and other Plymouth volunteers. She also noted that he was a tireless reader with an "exhaustless fund of knowledge of interest to boys, from history, invention, electricity, and mechanical engineering. When he told a story, if it be from the Bible, from mythology or from the life of some historic character, he held the attention of the boys as no other speaker could." Finally, Mrs. Ritchie recalled that his love for music and his beautiful tenor voice inspired the boys, for

Members of the George Colman Boys' Club enjoy swimming, boating, and the camaraderie of this summer outing at Horsehead Bay in the early 1920s.

whom singing was always a joy. "With Oscar Marsolais, a genius at the piano, the church rocked to the strains of 'Throw Out the Life Line' or 'Wake! Wake! Wake and Greet the Day!' "

Following Mr. Colman's death in 1933, his old friend Judge Everett Smith wrote to Laurence Colman: "No one can estimate in this life the values in character building that he (George) helped to create in hundreds of boys, for the most part recruited from the underprivileged groups downtown . . . many now influential in mature years, will hold him in grateful, loving, and reverent remembrance."

The work passed from Mr. Colman's long term of leadership to the Boys' Work Committee. In 1943, it transferred management of the program to the Rotary Youth Foundation. That year's *Annual Reports* recorded that the Rotary planned to use the YMCA gymnasium and swimming pool for physical education and sports and would continue to conduct small group meetings, manual-training classes, and Sunday afternoon "very inspirational religious services" at Plymouth.

In 1946, the Rotarians expanded the program substantially by affiliating themselves with the Boys' Club of America,

George Colman (second row at left with hand on boy's shoulder) poses with club members and some of their friends and adult leaders on the steps of Plymouth.

a character-building organization for youth that at the time was headed nationally by former President Herbert Hoover. Finally in 1954, the Rotarians moved the Boys' Club into a building of its own. It had been at Plymouth for 55 years.

International Outreach

In the late 1890s while George Colman was starting the program for street boys, gold was discovered in the Klondike. Seattle suddenly became the gateway to Alaska. All sorts of suppliers, transport services, and schemers moved to the city to capitalize on the steady stream of prospectors, adventurers, dreamers, and their entourage.

At Plymouth several men and a few women caught gold fever and hastily booked passage aboard crowded steamers to rush northward. Discreet reports in the *Herald* do not mention whether members of "our Klondike contingent" struck it rich; but they do tell of safe returns and also of the less-fortunate Deacon E. K. Hill whose two sons returned without him.

Recognizing the need for moral and spiritual guidance in the boom-or-bust mining towns, Plymouth helped establish

Congregational churches in Alaska. Judge Wood initially went north in search of gold and made several return trips, taking with him Bibles, hymnals, and other materials in support of church work. His wife, Emma, occasionally joined him to promote Congregationalism and the related work of the Women's Christian Temperance Union.

Along with transcontinental railroads and the Alaska gold rush, the 1890s witnessed our country's declaration of war against Spain. As a strategic Pacific Coast port, Seattle quickly mobilized to accommodate incoming and outgoing troops and supplies. Women throughout the city formed the Pacific Northwest's first Red Cross Society. As in wars to come, they had the support of their churches, where they met to sew comfort bags and knit bandages. They also made every effort to give "our boys" a proper send-off and homecoming.

Captain George H. Fortson of Company B, First Washington Volunteers, was active in Plymouth. He attended services on Easter Sunday, 1898, with his troops to hear Dr. Temple's sermon, "Christ, the Leader and Commander." The captain was mortally wounded in the Philippines nearly two years later, and Dr. Temple eulogized him before what the *Herald* called an "immense and patriotic throng" at the Seattle Armory. Following return of the troops, the Fortson Relief Corps named in honor of the fallen captain gave a musical and literary program at Plymouth, exotically entitled "Evening in Manila."

Unified under the great American and British mission boards, the turn-of-the-century goal of churches and Christian Endeavor societies was "the evangelization of the world in this generation." At Plymouth interest in foreign missions had grown considerably. In 1898, the congregation formed the Church Missionary Society, replacing the former Women's Missionary Society that had been active since the 1880s. Perhaps because of Seattle's increased involvement in international affairs, the congregation now wanted a more personal contact with the foreign field. Through the American Board of Commissioners of Foreign Missions, Plymouth in 1904 agreed to support its own missionaries, the first of whom were the Reverend and Mrs. Emery W. Ellis.

Since 1885, the American Board had sent missionaries to

the populous city of Lintsing in the Shantung Province of northern China. Despite the bloody Boxer Rebellion in 1900 to oust foreigners, a small but dedicated following of native Chinese sought the "Jesus way." Emory and Minnie Case Ellis were assigned to this poor, remote area.

They spent three weeks enroute in Seattle where Mr. Ellis celebrated his ordination at Plymouth. Expressing support, enthusiasm, and a fascination for the lure of the mysterious Orient, youth and adult groups joined in fellowship with the Ellises, giving them a rousing send-off on "Ladies' Night" at the Men's Club. Club president John Schram gave the warm farewell speech. He was also president of the Seattle Chamber of Commerce and earlier in the day had presented $10,000 in citizen donations to the Moran Brothers Company to subsidize building of the battleship Nebraska.

In accordance with Plymouth's sponsorship of Emory and Minnie Ellis, Dr. Temple invited the American Board of Commissioners for Foreign Missions to have its annual meeting in Seattle. Plymouth members gladly extended their hospitality to the delegates in 1906. In addition to representatives from all parts of North America, missionaries came from Japan, India, Micronesia, Hawaii, and northern China.

Dr. Temple was not present to greet them. He closed his 10-year pastorate in 1905 to accept the call of Plymouth Church of Cleveland, Ohio. He reasoned that the change would be beneficial to both the Seattle congregation and himself.

The Reverend Dr. Samuel M. Freeland as interim pastor stepped in to host the meeting. He and his wife, Elizabeth, had come to Seattle and Plymouth to join their daughter Elizabeth Freeland Curtis. A retired Congregational minister, he filled many pulpits in times of need and, according to Mrs. Rayner's account, came to be called "the Congregational Bishop of the Pacific Coast."

Plymouth took its new, personalized commitment to the missionary field very seriously. Members corresponded regularly with the Ellises and learned about their very primitive living conditions and about their work. With Anson Burwell as chairman of the Benevolence Committee, Plymouth annually sent thousands of dollars to Lintsing where the mission community expanded with new schools, a church, houses, and a hospital. When the Ellises only child died at age two, the Seattle congregation sent a bell for the Lintsing church tower in his memory. In 1908, Plymouth decided to double its commitment by sponsoring Vinton and Florence Cutler Eastman as additional missionaries to Lintsing.

While on furlough to America, Mrs. Ellis discovered a revived interest in tatted trimming and determined to teach use of the shuttle to impoverished Chinese women at the mission. As a result, women enrolled in her mission classes were over the years able to export tatting and earn substantial funds. In cooperation with the Red Cross, the mission also helped create job opportunities for men. They were organized into road-building crews and given rations in return for their work. Plymouth's allegiance to the Lintsing mission was still strong when in 1921 the area was devastated by famine. Fund-raising efforts in response included dinners and bazaars organized by the Women's Association and benefit performances staged by Christian Endeavor societies.

In 1924, the church sponsored one of its own, Valley Nelson, who as a registered nurse took charge of the women's department at Lintsing Memorial Hospital. The facility had neither electricity nor running water but was said to be the only modern medical center in an area inhabited by more than 5 million people. Plymouth members maintained active and caring correspondence with her and continued to donate funds and supplies until her work was cut short by World War II.

In addition to Lintsing, the church's growing international awareness prompted its sponsorship of missionaries to other countries, including Iraq, India, Greece, and the Philippines. Like Valley Nelson, several missionaries were members of Plymouth and, as such, their missions evoked a deeply personal sensitivity within the congregation.

Women's Suffrage

Perhaps the most evident sign of early Seattle's growing international awareness was the city's enormously successful world's fair in 1909 on the University of Washington campus.

With generous allocations from the state and the city, the Alaska-Yukon-Pacific Exposition brought stunning landscaping and needed buildings to the campus that had heretofore consisted of only two academic halls and two student dormitories. While attracting numerous visitors to the region, the fair also brought United States and world attention to Seattle and greatly enhanced the city's position in international trade.

Plymouth was busy during the fair hosting numerous national and regional organizations that planned their conventions in conjunction with the exposition. One group that brought its luminaries to Seattle was the National Women's Suffrage Association. Plymouth members had a history of advocating women's enfranchisement and hoped to garner support for the issue that was once again to be presented to male voters in Washington State in the 1910 election.

Though united in purpose, members of the state's delegation to the association's convention were at odds in terms of strategy. A power struggle ensued between the flamboyant May Arkwright Hutton who led the Spokane delegation and the more conservative Emma Smith DeVoe whose following came from the western side of the state. Because of their internal bickering, Washington's delegates were reprimanded and ultimately denied the right to vote at the convention. The newspapers had a field day. One satirical reporter fabricated a story that the Spokane delegation had been locked in the back room of Plymouth Church and that the disgruntled women were forced to make their escape by climbing through a window. When the national press misconstrued the fiction as fact, Plymouth's "back room" gained widespread notoriety.

In spite of the fracas, Washington women won the coveted vote in 1910. With the support of churches and other organizations advocating reform, the newly enfranchised women immediately began turning the tide in city politics. Mayor Hiram Gill had opposed dry laws and befriended brothel owners. He was recalled, an action that dealt sin in the city a vigorous blow. Reform candidate George Cotterill (later an active member of Plymouth) defeated Mr. Gill in his bid for reelection.

Building Again

At the turn of the century, tree-lined Third Avenue with its wooden sidewalks and unpaved street was still an almost pastoral setting and the home of several churches. The neighborhood was, however, undergoing rapid change. The federal government had purchased the half block next to Plymouth for a new post office, and the University of Washington had signed a 50-year lease with the Metropolitan Building Company to develop the school's downtown property as a long-term producer of income. Influenced by the architectural ideals of the city-beautiful movement, elaborate plans for the University Tract included the Cobb Building directly adjacent to Plymouth and the nearby White-Henry-Stuart Building. Along with new construction, the city's ambitious plans to recontour the land to better commercial advantage would completely disrupt the neighborhood.

All of Plymouth sensed the urgency of paying off the lingering $30,000 debt to prepare for the future. In early 1901, however, the trustees decided to postpone their own fund-raising drive in deference to that of the YMCA to which Plymouth members donated $10,500. These contributions seem to have worked as a catalyst for church members. They quickly pledged the needed $30,000 to Plymouth, payable within the next six months. In July the congregation packed the sanctuary, triumphantly singing the doxology as James Moore, chairman of the Board of Trustees, touched a match to the mortgage papers. With Plymouth free of debt, the trustees decided to hire Julia Low as the church's first secretary.

By 1905, the ivy-covered, red-brick church was no longer modern or unique, and in the eyes of some of its members, it had even lost its charm. Shepherded by the dynamic Reverend Dr. Mark Matthews, the Presbyterians reigned supreme with a fine new church and an outstanding pipe organ. In addition, long-anticipated regrading operations were taking place throughout the University Tract. Plymouth's foundation was soon to be a floor above the surrounding modern business district.

Amidst dust, din, and disarray, members greeted their new pastor, the Reverend Dr. Francis Van Horn, who arrived with

Billed as "the Scenic Hotel of the World," the Washington Hotel (in background) enjoys a commanding view from the crest of Denny Hill. It was owned by Plymouth's James Moore who, with many supporters, resisted demolishing the structure until they were convinced that level streets would be good for business in Seattle. Like other buildings along Third Avenue, Plymouth (center right) needed a makeshift stairway for access during regrading operations.

his wife, Lois, in the summer of 1906. Together they weighed their options, concluding almost from the start that Plymouth would need a new building. Should they remain where they were in the heart of the burgeoning business district? If so, they would have to tear down their building and regrade the lot so that it would be on the same level as the rest of the neighborhood. Or should they sell their valuable property and move to another downtown lot or to a less-expensive site in a nearby residential neighborhood?

All of the unspiritual talk about politics, business, and material progress bothered the new pastor who in an issue of the *Herald* early in 1909 pleaded with his congregation: "Let us ask God to make us into a new church worthy of a new 'house of prayer.' " Dr. Van Horn lamented the unenviable task of trying to lure his far-flung congregation into the muddy, dredged-out neighborhood that surrounded the church: "I am

The Reverend Dr. Francis Van Horn, 1906–1914

tired of rainy Sundays, aren't you? I am tired of everything that keeps people away from church: weather, laziness, indifference, the world, the flesh, the devil. . . . Why not pack old Plymouth anyway to show we are in earnest? Meantime, I'm going over to Spokane to hear Billy Sunday. I want to see 8,000 people crowding in nightly to hear a sermon. I want to hear the man on the street talking religion instead of politics or business. . . ."

In an effort to bolster attendance at weekly prayer meetings, the women in 1908 expanded their Thursday evening dinner program for schoolteachers so that anyone who wanted to remain downtown could enjoy an affordable 15-cent meal. So great was the response that the Women's Association hired Julia Proctor as chief cook, a post she efficiently and cheerfully held until her retirement in 1936. With resourceful volunteers, she prepared the meals in a small, dimly lit basement kitchen equipped with little other than rough board shelves and a rusty iron range. Nonetheless, the dining room grew more and more crowded, and Dr. Van Horn's prayers for better attendance at weekday services were answered.

So popular were the dinners that the pastor and trustees decided to invite the entire membership to a New Year's fellowship banquet. When an unprecedented 425 people accepted the invitation, the church needed help. Members borrowed tables from the YWCA and the YMCA and crowded them as closely as possible in the basement assembly room. Hostesses who presided at each table brought linens and silver from home, and the Stone-Fisher Company loaned the dishes. Because the church kitchen was so inadequate, the women did most of their cooking at the YWCA, and Plymouth young people transported the food to the church and waited tables.

A year later in 1909, Plymouth had its second all-church dinner to celebrate its 40th anniversary. This event initiated a new Plymouth tradition: the annual dinner that has since occurred each January in conjunction with the annual meeting.

Despite Dr. Van Horn's professed disdain for "the unspiritual talk of politics and business," he soon acceded to the voices of progress. The transition from the second to the third Plymouth building was a long and complicated odyssey. In 1906, members voted to accept an offer of $350,000 for their property at Third Avenue and University Street and to move out of the downtown area to the corner of Harvard Avenue and Union Street where they could obtain a lot for $67,000. A Chicago architectural firm was hired to draw up plans for a large Gothic church to be constructed of stone.

As a result of their intended move from premium downtown property, the trustees foresaw a new debt-free church with a remaining bank balance of approximately $100,000. Their plan as outlined by Mrs. Rayner was to use the extra money not for Plymouth Church but for "missionary and benevolent enterprises for the upbuilding of Christ's kingdom under Congregational auspices." Among those to receive assistance were the Japanese American Congregationalists who

By 1911, Plymouth was ready to yield its site at Third Avenue and University Street to encroaching commerce, as evidenced by the new Cobb Building at right.

wanted to organize their own church with a Japanese-speaking pastor. When the University Congregational Church began its fund-raising drive for a new building, Plymouth donated $10,000.

Ultimately, this donation was to cause Plymouth's congregation considerable hardship because the economic panic of 1907 forced purchasers of the downtown property to renege on their contract. In 1908, trustees decided to make the best of what they had—to clean up the old building and add the annex that was to be used by the George Colman Boys' Club and the Christian Endeavor societies. In what the press called a "high ethical spirit," the church agreed to take back the title to its downtown property and to return the $85,000 received so far in payments from the destitute investment company.

In an attempt to adapt to their changing neighborhood, the forward-thinking trustees considered constructing a five-story business building with shops and offices on lower floors and auditorium, sanctuary, and other church rooms on higher levels. (This concept would surface again in 1960.) Another option was the Harvard Avenue and Union Street site. Finally in 1910, Plymouth decided instead to accept an offer of $325,000 from theater developer Alexander Pantages for the downtown property and also the lot at Harvard and Union. Members voted unanimously to purchase the half block at Sixth Avenue and University Street on the east side of the University Tract where Plymouth still stands today.

In the final months at the old building, former pastors returned to reminisce and to remind the congregation of its already-impressive accomplishments. Plymouth vacated the building in April. Mr. Pantages leased it to the Salvation Army for a summer of revival services and then had it demolished to make way for his opulent Palomar Theater. Plymouth members accepted the hospitality of friends, worshiping on Sundays in the new YMCA auditorium and having Thursday evening prayer meetings at the YWCA. While doing their best to maintain regular church programs, they looked forward to a new decade that would open with the excitement and challenge of building.

3
The Progressive Era 1910–1920

Within this decade the few remaining downtown homesteads would become history, yielding to the progress of urbanization. Neighborhoods would grow as Seattleites relinquished the core of their city to commerce.

Plymouth would adapt to an enlarged Seattle by widening its definition of community and cooperating with other major congregations to retain the Church as the social and spiritual center. During the decade, Plymouth— along with the city and country—would also be called upon to find its footing in the tempest of World War I.

Among Plymouth members who contributed substantially to Seattle's outward expansion were Judge Wood and Dr. Kilbourne who just before the turn of the century had figured in bringing electric railways to Seattle. These railways were particularly important in connecting the Fremont, Aurora, and Green Lake areas to downtown. In east Wallingford and the treeless Capitol Hill area north of Volunteer Park, James Moore platted some of the city's most fashionable neighborhoods.

After the turn of the century James Colman, owner of the Yesler Mill Company on Union Bay, cooperated with his son, Laurence, to clear virgin timber from large areas east and west of the University of Washington. Major Hiram M. Chittenden of the U.S. Army Corps of Engineers designed the Ballard Locks and the ship canal that in 1917 cut through land barriers to link Puget Sound, Lake Union, and Lake Washington, lowering the latter by nearly 20 feet.

While Plymouth members participated in the outward migration, they also remained steadfastly devoted to downtown Seattle. Many made frequent and often-difficult trips to Plymouth. Some came from Laurelhurst by boat to Madison Park and then by streetcar to downtown. Others braved the rutted dirt roads that motor cars still shared with horse-drawn surries. They made the journey because Plymouth offered a means of participating in the central life of the city. With the spreading of the metropolitan area, the downtown church continued to grow in influence; both old and new members represented newly developed residential areas.

Classic Design in a Time of Modesty

At first, status consciousness was unknown in the outlying neighborhoods, and privacy was not a priority. A logger's shack or an immigrant farmer's vegetable patch could well be next door to an elaborate mansion. Roger Sale in *Seattle: Past to Present* notes that the wealthy who moved to view property near the turn of the century all tried to face toward the city, admiring the enclave that they had wrested from the natural environment.

Sale observes: "All this was to change quite quickly in the next 10 or 15 years, when the 'democratic' mixing of rich and bourgeois and settled poor was replaced by a more self-conscious sorting out of neighborhoods into good and not so good. At that time the commanding view of the city was given up for a house less easy to spot from the street or the streetcar and whose view was of a lovely garden in the backyard, of water and mountain."[1]

Plymouth boards and committees took this change into account as they worked on plans for a new building. It was a time of modesty; opulent facades were considered garish and in poor taste. It was also a time marked by Progressives and Populists with their moral-reform priorities, by labor unrest, political bouts between monopolists and Democrats, and World War I. Internally and externally, then, Plymouth's building plans were strongly influenced by the professed modesty of the rich as well as by the practical reformist and democratic positions of many of its members.

1. Roger Sale, *Seattle: Past to Present* (Seattle: University of Washington Press, 1976), 60.

Combined with the times, the years of dreaming, deliberating, and fantasizing over all sorts of architectural options must have had a sobering effect on the congregation. Unlike the building committee of 1906 that had opted for a stone structure of Gothic design, the committee of 1910 led by Laurence Colman chose to avoid a hint of external ostentation.

After reviewing designs submitted by several competing architects, the committee recommended those of John Graham, Sr., a Seattle architect who was no doubt in tune with the times. The scheme called for a "plain, chaste example of classic architecture, as adapted to church purposes by the English in the time of the Reformation, peculiarly characteristic of New England . . . a true Congregational church without ornamentation save for the pillars, which are essential to the type and the tower, or more properly, belfry, which in due time should contain a set of memorial chimes." The architect apparently felt compelled to justify any perceived frills by adding that "the tower proclaims it to be a church."[2]

If the exterior were to appear austere, the interior by contrast was designed to welcome and serve multitudes. The sanctuary would have a seating capacity of 1,400 (including the balcony) with an additional 65 seats in the choir; the Sunday school rooms would accommodate 800 scholars. The dining room would seat 250 and could be doubled by opening doors to other rooms. The modern, restaurant-equipped kitchen could serve 500 meals at a time. Also included were a library, church office, pastor's study, a five-room apartment for the custodian, separate parlors for women and men, manual-training shops, and a gymnasium with a dressing room, showers, and lockers for 300 boys or girls. It was a building that the forward-thinking congregation did not intend to outgrow.

The interior of the church was elegant, with extensive use of polished woods, marble, and luminous chandeliers. The charming and beautiful appointments of the church parlors were credited to May W. Raser, then head of the Women's Association and an authority on colonial furnishings.

2. *Congregational Washington*, vol. 1, no. 2 (Seattle: Washington Congregational Conference, Inc., June, 1912).

Several contemporary Plymouth members who were youngsters in that church remember the magnificent leaded-glass ceiling in the sanctuary and the thrill of climbing around in the off-limits area above it. Fred Betts joined the church in 1919 and candidly recalls, "When I was able to avoid having to go to the services at 11 o'clock, I used to go up above the choir loft behind the organ where we weren't supposed to be—over all that glass." Fortunately, the brave did not perish; no one ever fell through. Today the medallion of that leaded glass is preserved in the ceiling of the church chapel.

When the trustees tallied estimated expenses, they found that the new building would cost $75,000 more than the amount realized from the sale to Alexander Pantages. The cost of the proposed church building itself was estimated at $145,000 with an additional $30,000 for furnishings, including the magnificent organ to be built by the Ernst M. Skinner Company of Boston. A rousing fund-raising campaign ensued with two teams of 30 men each vying to outdo one another. When the funds were pledged, the Pilgrims led by Roy P. Ballard claimed victory over Anson Burwell's Natives by a margin of $535. As a tribute to the 391 donors of gifts ranging from $2 to $15,000, all of their names were placed in the cornerstone.

On July 30, 1911, a festive throng gathered to witness the laying of the cornerstone. Women in silks and elaborate hats and dapper men in bowties and bowlers stood amidst neighboring, wood-frame boarding houses, now gray with dust from regrading operations. They looked on as Dr. Van Horn and Laurence Colman set the cornerstone. Frank Curtis, chairman of the Board of Trustees, gave the historical statement, and ministers from neighboring churches extended their good wishes. Former Plymouth minister Dr. Temple returned to pronounce the benediction.

By the end of the year, the congregation was able to have services in the almost-completed Sunday school area of the church where separate classrooms opened out into a large central hall that unified the entire space. From the start the new building was humming with activity; programs were scheduled every evening during that first week. At the annual meeting in January, 540 people sat down to dinner in the

The Reverend Dr. Mark A. Matthews from First Presbyterian addresses the crowd gathered on July 30, 1911, for the laying of the cornerstone. The resulting structure would dominate the neighborhood of wooden homes and boarding houses.

commodious new dining room and eagerly anticipated the advent of services in the sanctuary.

In March, however, the *Herald* related: "All Plymouth people have been hoping to enter the new auditorium with rejoicing on Easter Day, but alas! the organ is snowed up somewhere in blizzardy Kansas. . . . We must possess our souls in patience, in the meantime making the best of such blessings, as we have." Finally in May, capacity audiences flocked to the sanctuary to hear Dr. Van Horn's sermons, the choir, and the long-awaited, magnificent new organ.

Following the dedication service at which the Reverend Dr. Luther R. Dyott of Portland preached the sermon, Plymouth hosted an open house, inviting the public for music, refreshments, and athletics, and proudly proclaiming "136 doors—All open."[3] In addition to the manual-training shops and the gymnasium, members took special pride in their new Sunday school facilities that for the first time were large enough for a

3. Alice E. Rayner, *The Path We Came By: A History of Plymouth Congregational Church* (Seattle, 1937), 83.

Massed choirs fill the Plymouth chancel for this Christmas-time service in 1913.

completely graded school. The third floor of the Sunday school with its sky-lit assembly room accommodated the new junior department organized by Lucy E. Matthews whom Dr. Van Horn had recruited from his former church in Worcester, Massachusetts. The Men's Club and the Women's Association welcomed guests in their respective parlors (renamed in the 1950s the Elder Brewster Room and the Mayflower Room). In an article about the new church, the Washington Congregational Conference unabashedly proclaimed Plymouth "the best equipped Protestant Church on the Pacific Coast, and surpassed by none in the land."

With the new organ, the talented Judson Waldo Mather enhanced Plymouth's ministry as church organist and choirmaster, not only directing the music but also working with the Men's Club to organize public concerts in the sanctuary. The pews were equipped with seat numbers so that tickets could be sold for special concerts that featured locally and internationally acclaimed artists. Among the latter was Vladimir Horowitz who in the 1920s came to Plymouth for what was said to have been one of his early recitals.

For the Women's Association, the modern kitchen was the primary source of income. It produced an estimated 12,280 meals during the first year. One commentator spoke of the dining room as the "religious Waldorf-Astoria of America," where a tasty dinner was made all the more attractive with a bill of only 20 cents. Because the women were still struggling to pay their $5,000 pledge to the building fund, they eventually had to raise the price.

As another successful and innovative fund-raising activity, the Women's Association introduced the Literary Tea, one of Seattle's earliest book-review programs. Sponsored by the Queen Anne and Madrona circles, Mrs. Alvah Lemuel Carr delivered a series of three talks on English and American authors of the day. These programs proved to be popular and so lucrative that for years the women continued to sponsor something similar every spring.

Extension and the Unity Churches

As Plymouth grew, so did her progeny among Congregational churches in Seattle and the region. In 1913 at the 15th Triennial Council of Congregational Churches in Kansas City, Dr. Van Horn spoke on "The Religious Outlook on the Pacific Coast." It was at this historic conference that the Council adopted a new constitution and declaration of faith.

The following year the Reverend Clarence R. Gale, superintendent of the Seattle Congregational Extension Society, presented a lantern slide show on "Plymouth Church—Her Children and Grandchildren," the text of which is preserved in the church's archives. Mr. Gale talked extensively about Pilgrim on Capitol Hill that 15 years before was a struggling mission relying heavily on Plymouth and was now one of the leading churches in the state. Among other Seattle Congregational churches that were founded or substantially assisted by Plymouth, he itemized University, Edgewater, Queen Anne, Prospect, Green Lake, Keystone, Beacon Hill, Brighton, Columbia, West Seattle, Alki, Bayview, Olivet, Fairmount, Fauntleroy, Oak Lake, plus a number of distant missions.

In addition, he noted that Plymouth had helped the city's four Congregational churches where foreign languages were spoken: First German, Japanese, Norwegian, and Finnish. Mr. Gale reported that all "have pastors and are doing aggressive work among their people."

In a similar tone the Reverend Dr. Adna T. Leonard of Seattle First Methodist is quoted in a fall 1914 issue of the *Herald:* "The Congregation at Plymouth is one large family, and they have sent out of their strength many members to one suburb and another, until their children, represented by prosperous church buildings and congregations are to be found all over the Northwest."

One of the hallmarks of Dr. Van Horn's pastorate was his contribution to the spirit of ecumenical cooperation among Seattle's four central Protestant churches, all of which now conducted services in fine new buildings. During the Lenten season, the four "Unity" churches had a "Unity Campaign" to address common goals. On Thanksgiving Day they cooperated by exchanging choirs and pastors and on other occasions they worked together to host a series of evangelistic services.

The original "Unity" pastors were the Reverends Dr. Carter Helm Jones of First Baptist, Dr. Adna T. Leonard of First Methodist, Dr. Mark A. Matthews of First Presbyterian, and Dr. Francis Van Horn. Plymouth further enhanced the ecumenical movement by hiring the Reverend E. A. King who was considered an outstanding leader of young people in Christian Endeavor. The organization had been founded by Congregationalists but was by this time an interdenominational program.

Sparked by the fervor of ecumenism, Laurence and George Colman in 1914 purchased Seabeck on Hood Canal, a semi-deserted, former lumber town that they planned to convert to Christian conference grounds. Within a year the old mill houses, the hotel, and the community center were renovated so that Pacific Northwest churches and other religious organizations could begin to have retreats, meetings, and summer camps in the serene and beautiful setting. Maintained by the

Colman family for a number of years, Seabeck is still a popular conference center today.

In the spring of 1914 after eight years at Plymouth, Dr. Van Horn submitted his resignation. Now known as a "builder of churches," he accepted a call to the First Congregational Church of Oakland, California, where members were preparing to build a new facility. On his last Sunday at Plymouth, the other "Unity" pastors let their own congregations go a little early so that they could come to Plymouth to pay tribute to their esteemed colleague. Dr. Matthews gave a short address, and the *Seattle Post-Intelligencer* quoted Dr. Leonard as saying: "In late times there has been a great drawing together of the churches of the city, of whatever denomination. In particular the union of the downtown pastors has been a noticeable factor. In the new phase of Seattle's devotional spirit, Dr. Van Horn has played a leading part . . ."

The Presbyterian Pastor From Cape Town

The Pastoral Committee searched far and wide for a new minister, and many applicants preached sermons at Plymouth that left the congregation uninspired. Other candidates were rejected without an interview for a variety of reasons: Some were too old, others were too expensive, and still others were rumored to be smokers—absolutely unacceptable for a minister in 1914!

Continuing their search, members seem to have been only remotely aware of the conflagration in Europe that was ignited in August by a gunshot on the Bosnian plains at Sarajevo. More pressing by far were local concerns, especially the church's escalating debt; the trustees had had to borrow to take up the slack of unpaid pledges. For the two competing teams in the every-member canvass, the European conflict at least provided inspiration. Historian Alice Rayner says: "They were known as the 'Submarines' and the 'Aviators,' appropriate enough, to be sure, since they must plumb deeper depths and rise to greater heights than ever before if Plymouth was to make financial ends meet."

A foremost requisite for the new pastor was that he be a

The Men's Club has fund-raising on the menu for this 1914 canvass dinner.

dynamic preacher capable of filling the huge new sanctuary. Following an exhaustive search, Anson Burwell and his committee came up with a surprising recommendation: a Presbyterian minister from Cape Town, South Africa, who had never preached in America. A growing sense of internationalism may have influenced Plymouth when members voted unanimously in November to call the Reverend Hugh Gordon Ross. He promptly accepted and notified the expectant congregation that he would be in the pulpit by February.

Despite the danger of German submarines in the Atlantic, he journeyed by way of his native Scotland. Responding to the many letters he had received from people at Plymouth, he wrote from there: "I . . . almost feel 'at home' in America already. I have no idea where I should live when I arrive, but probably some of you will advise me when I come. Meantime I am coming alone, leaving my wife and children here with their grandparents."

Plymouth's Judge Jeremiah Neterer, Dr. Edward Lincoln Smith, and Fred Smith traveled by train to New York to welcome Mr. Ross to the United States and escort him across the country to his new parish. They were taken aback to find a man wearing plus fours and smoking a calabash pipe, a la Sherlock Holmes. The new minister was a far cry from previous non-smoking preachers! The delegation brought him on to Seattle anyway, and his wife and children later joined him.

The mood of eager anticipation was no doubt mixed with trepidation as Plymouth members assembled in their pews on a February Sunday in 1915 to have their first glimpse of Mr. Ross. Evidently he passed muster by conveying the desired impression. Mrs. Rayner records that someone said his "prayer didn't stop at the ceiling." She further recalls that "He preached with fire . . . a very passion of earnestness. And his background of scholarship, gained in the thorough British manner, made every word he uttered worthy of the closest attention."

A Bible scholar, Mr. Ross relied on the Good Book as a guide to everyday life. Wives and mothers enthusiastically participated in his women's Bible class on Wednesday mornings at which they dealt with the multiple problems of homemaking. In addition to this class, Mr. Ross also conducted a popular course in Bible study at the University of Washington with several hundred students in attendance.

After the Ross family was comfortably ensconced in its Capitol Hill home, Mrs. Ross established her own hospitality program, further drawing people together. Once a month she hosted an informal afternoon and evening open house for Plymouth people at which she always served a proper English tea.

In an effort better to acquaint himself with his parish, the new pastor instituted the Plymouth Council, a body composed of the minister and assistants, the clerk, senior deacon and deaconess, presidents of church organizations, and leaders of departments, committees, and boards. The Council met monthly to discuss various concerns and to be a clearinghouse for ideas.

Mr. Ross had a strong interest in missionary activities and wrote in a spring 1915 issue of the *Herald* that Plymouth's reputation as a missionary congregation was the chief factor in his decision to come to Seattle. He had already felt the tragedy of the war in Europe when his brother perished on a torpedoed ship. Now the pastor must have been frustrated by his congregation's apathy, undoubtedly influenced by the United States' position of neutrality. Through missionary

The Reverend Hugh Gordon Ross, 1915–1918

agencies, Mr. Ross was at least able to arrange for a concert at Plymouth that raised $1,075 for the benefit of Armenian war victims.

The War To End All Wars

Despite his personal affinity for European affairs, Mr. Ross kept all mention of the war out of his sermons until April 7, 1917, when the United States declared war against Germany. On that Easter Sunday a stunned congregation listened to an impassioned sermon on "War and the Risen Christ" as the jubilant Mr. Ross celebrated what he considered to be the salvation of Europe and possibly the world. He proclaimed a week later in the *Herald* that, for the duration of the war, each service would close with the singing of the last verse of the national hymn: "Our fathers' God, to Thee,/Author of Liberty/ To Thee we sing./Long may our land be bright/With freedom's holy light/Protect us by Thy might,/Great God, Our King."[4]

The *Herald* began publishing in bold type the "Plymouth Roll of Honor." It would steadily lengthen as more men enlisted. Included in the first wave of enlistees were the sons of Arn S. Allen, secretary of the YMCA, and Dr. Francis Van Horn. Mr. Ross viewed his stance in favor of U.S. entry into the war not as advocacy for hostility but rather as support for the restoration of world peace. This position generated a flood of protests that he steadfastly answered from the pulpit.

While citizens everywhere grappled with the ethics of war and peace, Mr. Ross forged ahead, emphasizing the necessity of the United States to defend the world against tyranny. His sermons (many of which were published in pamphlet form) bore titles such as "The Christian Ethic of War," "Love Your Enemies," "Our Homes at War," "America and the Allies," "A Kaiser in Israel," "The Price of Freedom," and "Can We Forgive Germany?"

He upheld the sword of justice and exhorted Christians to fight for the lofty goals of peace and freedom. At the same time, Mr. Ross was mindful of human frailty and of the special needs of people in crisis. Sympathizing with the soldiers in slaughterhouse trenches between France and Germany, the minister on one occasion urged a shocked congregation to send the men cigarettes because Bibles were already being dispensed in quantity. By the middle of June, anti-war protestors had generally fallen into line with Mr. Ross, demonstrating a patriotic fervor that proclaimed this war as a necessity to restore peace and to make the world safe for democracy.

The humanitarian role of churches in wartime was of vital importance to Mr. Ross and his parishioners who responded wholeheartedly to the appeal of Henry M. Suzzallo, president of the University of Washington and Seattle chairman of the Red Cross War Fund. A friend of Plymouth who had previously drawn large and enthusiastic audiences as a speaker at the Men's Club, Dr. Suzzallo in the spring of 1917 wrote an

4. "The Star Spangled Banner" became the national anthem in 1931. Prior to that time, patriotic gatherings commonly sang the national hymn.

open letter to Seattle's ministers. It read in part: "We ask you to stir the great heart of this city so that its generosity will create a complete organization of mercy back of the long battle lines of the world war. The need is urgent. The machinery of wounding is perfected far beyond the machinery of healing. . . . The government of the United States cannot care for the problem; it is a partisan in the war. But the people of America can . . ."

Plymouth people contributed to both governmental and humanitarian efforts. The following announcement appeared in dramatic boldface in a fall issue of the *Herald:* HAVE YOU SUBSCRIBED TO THE SECOND LIBERTY LOAN? REMEMBER! IF YOU HAVE MONEY TO SPARE IT IS YOUR DUTY AS A CHRISTIAN TO LEND IT TO THE GOVERNMENT!

Within a week after war was declared, the women of Plymouth had organized a Red Cross auxiliary with committees for sewing, knitting, and publicity. Custodians transformed the women's parlor into a Red Cross workroom by taking down the drapes, rolling up the rug, and bringing in long tables for sewing machines. On Tuesdays and Thursdays from 10:00 A.M. until 5:00 P.M., the women in their white aprons and headdresses pushed themselves to meet ambitious production goals. By March Plymouth Auxiliary had produced 913 pairs of socks, 213 sweaters, 354 hospital bed shirts, 3,559 surgical dressings of sphagnum moss, and 1,697 miscellaneous pieces. On Wednesdays the Daughters of the British Empire (many of whom were Plymouth members) used the facility for their Red Cross work. The Women's Association also prepared weekly public luncheons and turned the proceeds over to the Red Cross.

Throughout this period Plymouth people maintained contact with their missionaries in Lintsing, China, and did what they could to help. The Reverend Emory Ellis wrote from China in the fall of 1917: "People here are starving. Eating peanut shells, sweet potato vine, the refuse after oil is pressed from beans and nuts, leaves, grass, reeds, rushes, bark, twigs, etc. Tens of thousands are wandering about begging and stealing. Oh the pathos of it all . . . children abandoned and sold; houses torn down and trees cut down for fuel and general distress mark the regions that last Fall were devastated by the great floods of water . . ."

The Sunday school responded with a special offering that raised nearly $500, and the Women's Association sent boxes of provisions and additional funds. Dr. Susan Tallman was another of the missionaries; she wrote of her work as an organizer of labor battalions designed to give Chinese men employment as domestic road and bridge builders. To the consternation of the concerned congregation in Seattle, some of the battalions were being recruited for overseas service in support of the war.

Life on the Home Front

Not all of the war effort was directed overseas. On the home front churches were informally enlisted to play a very special part. In words of appeal and encouragement to churches carried in the *Herald* during the winter of 1918, Secretary of War Newton D. Baker said, "We cannot afford, when losing boys in France to lose children at home." Acknowledging the fact that the public schools did not offer religious training, he promoted vacation Bible school as a means of preserving the world and youth for democracy.

Plymouth took seriously the nonsectarian daily vacation Bible school with paid staff and volunteer instructors, storytellers, and administrators working with children between the ages of 8 and 13. Of the 100 students enrolled, only a few came from Plymouth families. The others were Episcopalian, Christian Scientist, Catholic, Presbyterian, Swedish Mission, Danish Lutheran, Baptist, Christian, Methodist, or unchurched. A sizeable group came from Mother Ryther's orphanage.

For four weeks the children's activities included Bible study, storytelling, manual training, music, and gym. The music department worked with the children to organize a vacation-school choir that proudly sang twice at Plymouth's Sunday evening services. Some of the boys went to the YMCA for their first experience at swimming. On Tuesdays and Thursdays, children learned about their city through excursions to its many parks where they enjoyed a variety of activities. Boys and girls from other churches were urged to attend their own Sunday schools on the Sabbath; but those who didn't belong to a church were always invited to Plymouth.

During the war years, the graded Sunday school also remained a high priority. Claude Eckart was its capable superintendent, and his devoted volunteer teaching corps numbered more than 100. Among them was Mrs. Charles Stoutenborough who so inspired the young women in her Bible class that, following her death in 1919, they formed the Stoutenborough Class, an organization that continued for years to attract new members. In addition to conducting religious-education classes, the Sunday school sponsored an accomplished junior choir and youth-fellowship programs, including the popular summer camp for boys.

With the assistance of a boys' work secretary, the manual-training rooms and the gymnasium remained open for group activity almost every evening. The sound of bouncing basketballs reverberated throughout the entire church as Ross George worked with the boys to develop winning teams. By 1918, the *Herald* was devoting an entire page to Sunday school notes, and the school itself published a 16-page pamphlet entitled *Plymouth Chimes*. Like the *Herald*, the *Chimes* gave stark testimony to the extent of Plymouth's involvement in the world crisis. The lists of wounded, missing, and dead grew longer. The roll of honor filled a page and a half and included names of men and women from almost every family in the church. Plymouth members were at Chateau Thierry, St. Mihiel, and in the Argonne, or less-specifically, "somewhere in France."

The young people joined efforts to help by sending goodie boxes, games, records, and books to Camp Lewis and the Bremerton Navy Yard and by offering their friendship to troops stationed in the Seattle area. Members of the Senior Endeavor Society attended dances and parties for enlisted men hosted by the YWCA and YMCA and, while there, they invited young soldiers and sailors to come with them to Sunday Christian Endeavor meetings at the church.

Preparations for the war brought thousands of newcomers to Seattle, and Plymouth made a concerted effort to provide

Dances at the YWCA for doughboys were on the social calendar of Plymouth young people. There they invited the servicemen to join them for Senior Christian Endeavor meetings at the church on Sunday evenings. (Courtesy the YWCA)

them with a church home. The "war budget" included funds to welcome the visitors, to publicize church programs, and to employ E. C. Knapp as the new director of religious education.

Peace, Praise, Pestilence, and Prayer

One of the most attractive features of Plymouth's program was its music that throughout the decade brought numerous visitors to the church. A winter 1918 issue of the *Herald* notes that, in addition to its regular part in the Sunday service, the choir "has given a goodly number of the best things along Cantata and Oratorio lines, and already has an enviable reputation throughout the Northwest as a choral society which does things.''

A review in that same issue of a wartime *Messiah* conducted by Choirmaster Mather reads:

> The elemental melodies of the choruses were sung with a fullness of tone that was inspiring and most creditable to this choir. Supplemented with an orchestra of eleven strings the ensemble of organ and chorus made the grand old oratorio live anew. The soloists were Mrs. Margaret Moss Hemion, soprano; Nellie B. Apfel, contralto; James Harvey, tenor; and Wilfred Worth, baritone. There was an excellence of interpretation that gave the whole performance a decided artistic effect and when the Hallelujah chorus was sung the audience showed its appreciation with generous applause. Plymouth was crowded and people stood throughout the entire program.

Having a full house in a sanctuary that seated 1,400 was not uncommon at Plymouth, which ranked at the forefront of the city's musical organizations. The church was by now paying its soloists as well as the choirmaster and organist. With the wartime depletion of the tenor and bass sections, the professional male vocalists proved particularly valuable. In addition to Sunday services and special performances, the soloists participated as guest artists in popular weekday organ concerts at the church.

In September 1918, Mr. Ross resigned to accept a call to a church in Massachusetts. He left behind a congregation that had matured through crisis and that was strongly united in its Christian mission. For the next two and a half years, Plymouth relied on interim pastors, most notably the Reverend Frederick Rouse and the Reverend J. B. Silcox.

Much of the credit for a smooth transition to a new senior minister belongs to church secretary Gertrude Seeley Evans who took a personal interest in all phases of the congregation's activities. As an exemplary church visitor, Lucinda Waite is said to have kept in touch with the entire membership, traveling to homes no matter how difficult they were to reach and admonishing stragglers to reenter the fold. During this period, Plymouth observed its 50th anniversary with

Plymouth's Emma Wallingford Wood and George Cotterill survey the site of the downtown YWCA during groundbreaking ceremonies in 1914. They were both for many years leading advocates of prohibition and clean government. When the photo was taken, Mrs. Wood was president of the YWCA and the Women's Christian Temperance Union and Mr. Cotterill was Seattle's mayor. Plymouth is visible at left. (Courtesy the YWCA)

considerable pomp, including visitations from former ministers and representatives from 20 "daughter" churches.

All of Seattle celebrated in the streets when on November 11, 1918, word came that the war was finally over. Its ravages lingered, however. People waited many months to hear of their loved ones, sometimes rejoicing with a soldier's return, sometimes receiving belated notification of death or injury, and in other instances hearing nothing at all.

Adding to the stress was the virulent international flu epidemic that reached Seattle in 1918 and persisted for more than a year. The congregation did its best to help the many families who were stricken by the sometimes-fatal virus. When the city banned public meetings in an effort to control the epidemic, Plymouth postponed a number of activities, including the training school for Sunday school teachers and the children's Christmas party.

Throughout the decade, the fear of vice in city hall, coupled with a disdain for monopolistic "interests," had forged an odd alliance. It included Suffragists, Populists, progressive Republicans, and Prohibitionists, all of whom had demanded social reform. Eternally in search of better pay and working conditions, organized labor was influenced by the Bolshevik Revolution in Russia, the rise of the radical Industrial Workers of the World (the "Wobblies") in neighboring farming communities and lumber camps, and the imminent paucity of jobs in a peacetime economy.

All of these factors contributed to the Seattle general strike that started on February 6, 1919. It was the first such stoppage in the nation. Aside from a few essential services, the streets of the city were empty for three days as workers stayed home. Mayor Ole Hanson threatened to call out the National Guard, union leaders ended the strike, and Seattle workers peacefully returned to their jobs as if nothing out of the ordinary had happened. The nonviolent strike had shown that labor unions could shut down the town; but without specific demands and with unclear goals, the strike had achieved nothing else. What followed were the disintegration of political and labor alliances and the end of an era in which social-reform priorities had engendered widespread support.

Plymouth identified its mission for the coming decade, however. A note in the *Herald* shortly after the new year began recapitulates and prophesizes: "The war has come and gone. The pestilence has waned. The strike has run its course. Red Cross, relief, and Liberty Loans have had their inning. . . . The church is now to have its turn."

4

The Roaring Twenties 1920–1930

Seattle's population had stabilized at just over 315,600 after a 25-percent increase during the previous decade. Creative energy was on the rise, nonetheless, and the twenties promised to be in many respects a turning point for the city and Plymouth. The new course would take the congregation into more liberal, activist territory as members interpreted the community-directed mission of an institutional church.

In 1920, the Boeing Airplane Company began to manufacture military aircraft in the "Red Barn" on the Duwamish River. A year earlier Bill Boeing and Eddie Hubbard had made aviation history by carrying mail in a Boeing Model C from Seattle to Vancouver, B. C. The airwaves hummed with transmissions from Seattle's first radio station, said to be the second in the nation. An opportunistic young truck driver named Dave Beck was hatching schemes that would lead to organization of the Teamsters union and his elevation to the formidable position of Teamster boss.

A Dynamic, Controversial Pastorate

Plymouth, too, was bursting with creative energy, eagerly awaiting a new senior minister after two and a half years with interim pastors. On a cold January evening in 1920, more than 400 members gathered for what promised to be a very special annual banquet. Suddenly, the jingling of a telephone bell hushed the animated throng. Holding the receiver to his ear, Judge Everett Smith announced that the caller was the Reverend Dr. Chauncey J. Hawkins, pastor of the First Congregational Church of Lowell, Massachusetts.

At a time when long-distance telephoning still made news and when connections were seldom clear, Judge Smith spoke loudly and clearly into the mouthpiece: "Hello, Dr. Hawkins? This is Judge Smith. I am speaking for Plymouth Church, Seattle. Do you hear me?"

Relating the answer to the congregation: "He said, 'Yes.' Dr. Hawkins, I am going to put the question of your election as pastor of Plymouth Church to a vote."

Judge Smith did so, and the congregation gave a resounding "Aye!"

"Did you hear?" asked Judge Smith. Again relaying the message to the congregation, "He heard!"

Dr. Hawkins continued, saying via his interlocutor: "I thank you folks very much for your offer. I hope that together we will do great work. I am sure that together we shall win."

The congregation responded with enthusiastic applause. Dr. Hawkins closed the conversation by stating that he would take up his new post on April 18.[1]

With the use of modern technology, Plymouth had embellished the phrase "extending the call" with the immediate transmission of the voice vote and the minister's acceptance over a distance of 3,500 miles. In the highest literary and dramatic sense, it foreshadowed the dynamic, often-controversial pastorate that was to come. True to the Roaring Twenties, Dr. Hawkins would raise the hackles of self-serving politicians and fundamentalist theologians and at the same time turn the church into one of the most expansive social and cultural centers in the city.

Considerable correspondence followed the historic long-distance call. Dr. Hawkins began immediately to work with the congregation and made some astute observations as he sized up his new flock. Mrs. Rayner quotes him as writing: "I am glad to see by the calendar you enclosed that the men are pushing the Bible Class. One thing is absolutely essential for a strong aggressive downtown church, namely a large body of aggressive and consecrated men. The women have a large and indispensible part to play, and it is seldom that they fail in

1. Alice E. Rayner, *The Path We Came By: A History of Plymouth Congregational Church* (Seattle, 1937), 111–12.

their responsibilities, but without a strong body of men who have the vision, enthusiasm, and faith, it is impossible to attempt to build a strong downtown church. From all I have been able to learn, Plymouth has such a group of men."

The Men's Club fell into inactivity during the war years but was not fully revitalized. Dr. Hawkins had rightly appraised the devotion of its members to the church and the downtown community. He may have underestimated Plymouth women, however. During his pastorate, they would launch the nondenominational Plymouth Girls' Club that would attract city-wide and national attention.

In preparation for his arrival in Seattle, Dr. Hawkins began to rouse the waiting congregation to activity, impelling members to recognize the potential of the Sunday evening service that at the time was poorly attended. Mrs. Rayner quotes him further: "Out of much experience I have reached the conviction that unless a downtown church can succeed in this service it will never reach a large number of the nonchurched population. The success of this service, however, will depend pretty much upon the vision of the people."

In his letter he urged each parishioner to "use every opportunity during the week to invite people to attend." He also made clear that he expected everyone to be on hand on Sunday evening so that they could greet and welcome strangers and introduce them to the new minister.

He concluded: "We can fill the church that first night, if your people will enter enthusiastically and wisely into their planning. I have seen it done. It is not mere theory. The beginning of a pastorate is the psychological opportunity, and that we must not let slip."

Rising to the challenge, Plymouth members actively promoted the forthcoming services, tantalizing friends and acquaintances with stories about their new pastor. Theologically, Dr. Hawkins was a modernist who endorsed the ethical and experiential aspects of Christianity and who broke with the dogmatic and creedal traditions propounded by fundamentalists (a label that, as defined at the time, fit almost all of Seattle's other Protestant preachers). For patriots and romanticists alike, Dr. Hawkins had the mystique of the legendary American hero. The son of Forty-Niners and a des-

The Reverend Dr. Chauncey J. Hawkins, 1921–1927

cendent of Daniel Boone, he was in his own right a noted north-woods explorer and hunter. A renowned photographer, he had also published popular stories of adventure for boys.

When Dr. Hawkins and his wife arrived in Seattle two weeks earlier than expected, he found a congregation skilled in promotion. His first services a week ahead of schedule attracted full houses morning and evening. So many people remained for the social hour that it had to be moved from the women's parlor into the spacious dining room. Of that occasion Mrs. Rayner notes, "This opportunity for strangers to meet church people and the minister over a friendly cup of tea was an innovation that achieved instant popularity."

At the May communion service one month after his arrival at Plymouth, Dr. Hawkins welcomed 85 new members into the congregation. As record crowds continued to come on Sunday evenings and as the membership continued to increase, a new vitality infused all aspects of church life with every department expanding its programs. The annual membership campaign of 1923 challenged every member—including the young people—to win a new convert for Plymouth.

Dr. Hawkins' drives for expansion were intended to promote spiritual and moral conviction and to impact the quality of life, not only within the church but also within the community. In a 1924 *Herald* he wrote: "We are not seeking crowds who desire merely to be entertained. People who look upon a church as they would upon a social club are not material upon which a church can be built. We are seeking people who desire to make their lives count for a better world, and who believe that the teachings of Jesus are the means through which a better world is to be made." To deliver his message to a larger public, Dr. Hawkins in 1927 established another Plymouth first: broadcasting his sermons over KOMO Radio.

Modernism Versus Fundamentalism

When Dr. Hawkins was installed as pastor of Plymouth in October 1921, every church that belonged to the Seattle ministerial association was represented. As pastor of Plymouth, he was considered the leading voice among Pacific Northwest Congregationalists. His installation address wherein he would explain his theological position drew widespread interest. Other ministers in the audience enthusiastically endorsed Dr. Hawkins' view that the message of the Gospel should be conveyed in contemporary language. As he continued, the nods of approval quickly changed to frowns of rejection.

Dr. Hawkins said: "I can't believe the God of this universe is less moral than a human parent. God does not have to be appeased like the evil spirits of the African savages. The sacrifice of the blood of the innocent is repulsive to all that is best in human nature." When he confirmed his belief that Christ's death was not a blood sacrifice intended to appease the wrath of an angry God, his conservative colleagues from other denominations recoiled.

In the evening following his installation, a hundred people met at the Swedish Tabernacle to hear a group of Seattle ministers denounce Chauncey Hawkins. As reported in the *Seattle Post-Intelligencer,* they assailed him for heresy and called him "dog," "coward," "hypocrite," "pagan," "blasphemer," and "no child of God." For the first time in years, no Thanksgiving "Unity" services were conducted among the downtown churches.

Plymouth's theological spectrum was broad, ranging from liberal to conservative. Violet Phelps Lewis was on the liberal side of the spectrum. Typical of her views was her parting advice as her daughter, Margarett "Missy" Fisher, stepped aboard the train for college: "Remember, Margarett, there are no absolutes." She had earlier answered a question about the immaculate conception by observing, "Well, Margarett, natural laws are immutable." Mrs. Lewis liked the controversial new minister from the start.

On the other end of the spectrum was Grace Bogue Betts. Fred Betts recalls, "My mother couldn't stand him!" She was a conservative and daughter of a Presbyterian minister. For her, Dr. Hawkins was entirely too radical.

Among the membership of Plymouth were others who questioned the beliefs of their new pastor. As Congregationalists, however, they regarded a divergence of opinion on theological points as less significant than the strong, constructive program of religious and social work in which they were engaged. They also endorsed the policy of an open pulpit which guarantees ministers the freedom to interpret how the Gospel applies to current events and problems.

Dr. Hawkins' most outspoken adversary by far was the fire-and-brimstone fundamentalist Dr. Mark Matthews of the neighboring First Presbyterian Church. In the pages of the *Seattle Post-Intelligencer,* Dr. Matthews proclaimed that the new minister and most of Plymouth Church were headed straight for hell. He preached sermons entitled "The Modern Heretic" and "The Modern Man Who Repudiates the Blood Atonement Is but an Ancient Pagan in a Tailored Suit."

Dr. Hawkins continued his teachings with sermons on "Premillenarianism and the Religion of the Modern Man" wherein he considered religion from the standpoint of social idealism. He preached: "The Bible is not an infallible and inerrant book. . . . It is not the revelation of God, but the record of a revelation that came through a course of human history." His views attracted many new members to Plymouth.

To refute Dr. Matthews and like-thinkers, Dr. Hawkins preached in October: "I have received scores of letters recently in which the writers undertake to prove the blood atonement by texts taken indiscriminately from all parts of the Bible. By this method of using Scripture a man can prove anything. He can prove that polygamy is a divine institution, as the Mormons did. He can prove that slavery is a divine institution as the old slave holders did. There is only one way to study the Bible—to look upon it as the record of a historical process, and then to study it to discover the evolution of ideas. It is intellectual suicide to study it any other way."

In that same sermon, Dr. Hawkins gave his endorsement to modern scholarship (including Darwinism) as a means of studying the Bible. The modernist/fundamentalist controversy erupted into heated debate in many parts of the nation. The most celebrated example was the 1925 "Monkey Trial" in which Tennessee schoolteacher John Scopes was convicted of defying state law to teach evolution.

Dr. Hawkins left no doubt regarding his own position: "How long can the church hope to hold the respect of thinking men when leaders of the church pronounce such evident falsehoods with all the authority of supernatural revelation, as we find in these clergymen who proclaim that only fools teach evolution? The pulpit of Plymouth Church not only accepts any truth established by the world of scholarship, but attempts to relate these truths to our practical living. People who are looking for a religion which can be made to harmonize with modern knowledge are invited to worship in this church."

The Sword of Righteousness

Despite their theological impasse, Dr. Matthews and Dr. Hawkins were politically united as outspoken leaders among

Seattle ministers who vowed to clean up the city. Anti-vice coalitions at Plymouth had long considered Dr. Matthews a staunch ally. His alliterative prescription for the redemption of humanity was "soap, soup, salve and salvation." In Seattle, this prescription rang out in periodic campaigns for municipal righteousness.

The push for prohibition that had claimed victory in Washington in 1916 and in the nation in 1919 had temporarily spent its supporters' energy. Recognizing their chance, vice mongers had moved quickly to make Seattle once again an open town. In the fall of 1921, Dr. Hawkins addressed the Young Men's Republican Club and declared, "If the police department of Seattle can't obtain law enforcement, the ministers of the city can and will." Brandishing "the sword of righteousness," he proceeded to file charges that led to an investigation of the city of Seattle by a King County grand jury.

In an attempt to divert public opinion and shift the blame, Mayor Edwin J. "Doc" Brown announced his defense plan at a December press conference. The *Seattle Post-Intelligencer* quotes the mayor:

> I'm going to tear the mask from these ministers and church members and church organizations who own property in the so-called vice districts. I'm going to have the police in the future report to me the names of the owners of buildings, the firms who lease the buildings for them, and all other matters in that connection, whenever the police arrest a bootlegger, a dope seller, or a disorderly woman. We'll see who is encouraging vice in this city. . . . No, I don't know whether or not Plymouth Church owns any of the property from which we have taken disorderly women or bootleggers. I'm not going to delve back, but in the future I'm going to bore in and tell the public all about it.

His promise went no further. He found no evidence to link Plymouth with "the Tenderloin."

The following spring Dr. Hawkins received threats of kidnapping and violence. In response the mayor ordered the women's protective division of the police department to guard him, observing in the pages of the *Seattle Union Record:* "But all Christians must expect to be persecuted. . . . I receive almost daily threats of some kind or other. The Bible proves persecution of Christians from the earliest times . . ."

Mayor Brown had grossly underestimated the power of churches and of women. When he went East in 1924, newly elected Councilmember Bertha Knight Landes took over as acting mayor. She immediately fired the chief of police and on a campaign platform of "municipal housekeeping" defeated Doc Brown in the 1926 election.

Mayor Landes was a former member of Plymouth who had transferred to the University Congregational Church in her neighborhood. As the first woman to be elected mayor of any major American city, she emphasized clean government, enforcement of prohibition, and the availability of wholesome recreation, all of which were strongly endorsed by Plymouth members. During the same period, Plymouth's George Cotterill, a former Seattle mayor, aspired to clean up the whole country but, as the Prohibition Party candidate, lost his bid for the presidency.

Since the historic Apple Orchard Convention at Plymouth in 1885, members of the congregation had continued to play leadership roles in temperance and anti-vice coalitions. In 1889, Mr. Cotterill had been the Grand Secretary of the International Order of Good Templars in Washington State and from 1905 to 1914 was Grand Templar of the United States. In 1914, Emma Wood had presided over the Seattle Chapter of the Women's Christian Temperance Union in which many other Plymouth women were active.

In his 1923 condemnation of Mayor Brown, Dr. Hawkins was quoted by the *Seattle Union Record* as saying: "Loggers and lumberjacks patronize the cheap dance halls because no other means of recreation is provided for them. . . . There is only one way to regulate the places which pander to the most brutish instincts of man. Cut out the cancer that is eating the heart out of Seattle. Eliminate the dance halls altogether. . . . Recreation must be provided for the workingman, but let it be spiritual recreation rather than a return to brutedom. The recreation must be unselfish, it must be educational, and it must tend to elevate the mind to higher things."

An Institutional Church

In line with modernistic theology, Dr. Hawkins emphasized making Plymouth an institutional church. The type of church toward which he was striving was aptly defined several years later by his successor, the Reverend Dr. L. Wendell Fifield:

> An institutional church differs from the normal type of church in that a considerable amount of its local program is designed and carried through to render Christian service to the community. A considerable portion of each year's budget of our church, which is indicated for local or current expenses, really goes for various forms of Christian community service. Because Plymouth is an institutional church, it is a center through which its members and friends can render a broad Christian service in the use of their time and money, rather than an organization seeking almost wholly to conserve and develop the spiritual interests of its members.

To this end, Dr. Hawkins and the congregation opened wide Plymouth's doors, creating an unprecedented array of new programs and utilizing its expansive facilities. Members zealously launched community-service programs as an active expression of Christian teachings. In addition to Sunday morning and evening services, the sanctuary did double duty when it became an auditorium during the week for concerts, conventions, and numerous other meetings of a religious, educational, or cultural nature. Sunday school rooms and the parlors were among other spaces used to accommodate smaller or less-formal gatherings.

A free health clinic in the church was developed as a result of Dr. Hawkins' attention to the synergistic affinity between health and religion. Early in his pastorate, he had devoted his Sunday evening sermons to the relationship of religion, health, and happiness and invited members of the audience to come to his office on weekday afternoons to discuss questions of life and religion. Mrs. Rayner quotes him as preaching, "We believe that religion is one of the vital factors of a life of power, health and happiness, and that many people suffer, bear unnecessary burdens, or miss the real joy of living, because they neglect religion, or do not know how to use it."

As more and more people responded, he decided that this was an area of real need. He consulted with a number of able psychologists, physicians, and dentists who agreed to assist him in establishing a free clinic within the church for those who were unable to pay.

Thus, the relationship between religion and science had taken a practical as well as a philosophical turn at Plymouth. The spiritual dimension likewise forged a new link with the arts when a free music school was opened in the church for talented young people who could not afford music lessons.

The Sunday school now had a regular morning worship service with Jean McMorran as leader. Children between ages 8 and 12 attended the "Junior Church" at which they had their own ushers, vested choir, and even a board of trustees to manage finances. Along with the children of members, Plymouth continued to look after the welfare of large numbers of boys and girls who lived downtown.

Encouraged by Dr. Hawkins and Associate Minister the Reverend Rudolph Ericson, both the Women's Association and the Men's Club sought to involve all of their members in some sort of church activity. For both organizations the high priority was youth work. Through dinners and bazaars the women raised funds to hire a girls' work secretary. The men sponsored a popular concert and lecture series to fund a secretary for boys' work that included the afternoon school for boys and the George Colman Boys' Club, now some 200 members strong. The extensive recreational, educational, and religious programs that evolved in both departments required the paid secretaries as well as a host of devoted volunteers.

The Plymouth Girls' Club

Under the energetic leadership of President Carrie L. Pike, the Women's Association hastened to develop programs for women and girls in the church and in the community. For Plymouth's teenaged girls, Augusta Burwell introduced the Puritan Maids. Dressed in the style of their New England forebears, they added a picturesque, vintage touch to church events at which they frequently helped. Following the pattern

Puritan Maids dressed the part when they helped with church functions.

of the women's circles, colonies of Puritan Maids later organized in different parts of the city so that girls could meet in their neighborhoods for wholesome recreation and religious instruction.

One of the most outstanding developments in the church was the Plymouth Girls' Club, a nondenominational organization for working women begun in 1921 under the leadership of girls' work secretary Marguerite Jorgensen. At the time, the YWCA was emphasizing social-service programs and physical fitness; but it was no longer a social and cultural center for women who worked downtown. Florence H. Oren, general secretary of the YWCA, knew how cold and austere the city could be for single women who had few acceptable avenues for social life. When she suggested organizing a club at the YWCA, the conservative board was unreceptive; so she turned her attention across the street to Plymouth.

Her suggestion fell on fertile soil. Although forced to retire because of ill health, Miss Jorgensen had planted a seed that with Mrs. Oren's dynamic leadership would grow into a premiere Seattle women's program, one that would be emulated in other cities throughout the nation.

Plymouth's dining room is packed for this typical gathering of the Girls' Club.

Monday evenings witnessed the transformation of the church dining room and parlors into a home for single working "girls" aged 18 to nearly 40.[2] Current Plymouth member Frances Penrose Owen was working then in personnel management at Frederick & Nelson and still exudes enthusiasm when she speaks of the Girls' Club: "Every Monday night business girls from all over the city came to Plymouth for a simple dinner, then singing which I conducted. I stood up on a chair and looked out over this congregation of more than 400 girls. There was a wonderful accompanist, Charlie Anderson, who could play almost any tune you could think of. After about 20 minutes of singing, the girls adjourned for classes."

By 1926, the membership had reached an astonishing count of 860 with interested women and men throughout the city donating their time and talents for class instruction. For an affordable $3 per year, payable in monthly installments,

2. During the twenties and thirties, single working women were called "girls." They were referred to as "women" when they married and when, if possible, they left a paid job to become a homemaker. For married women whose husbands could afford to support them, voluntary commitments were laudible; but to accept a paying job could have constituted an insult to their husbands.

any working woman could join the club, and for 25 cents could have dinner at the church.

Following the meal, a presentation by a speaker, and singing, members attended a variety of classes, described by Mrs. Oren as "a school of opportunity" that would strive to "teach everything that the girl needs to learn." Classes were offered in such subjects as literature, foreign languages, nature study, psychology, parliamentary law, personal budgets, arts and crafts, religious education, rhythmics, physical culture, basketball, glee club, and personality and charm. Current member Wilma Lowry taught a millinery class; enterprising businesswomen could also learn pattern design and dress-making so they could be stylish on a low budget.

Representatives from government, business establishments, art galleries, and social-service agencies addressed the popular "Know Your City" class. Among speakers for the "Art and Travel" class were University of Washington anthropologist Erna Gunther and Anna Louise Strong who for the past several years had lived in Russia. As a result of this class, some members arranged to go on excursions to Alaska, California, and Victoria, B. C.

One of the most memorable instructors was Lois Beil Sandall. She organized her drama students into theater groups called the "Plymouth Players" and the "Sandall Players," both of which performed at the church and for other community organizations. In 1918, she had formed the first church theater group in the country by recruiting drama students from the University of Washington to perform at Plymouth.

As a means of earning income, the Girls' Club sponsored popular performances of Mrs. Sandall's theater groups as well as concerts and guest speakers. In 1928 when Mayor Bertha Landes introduced Will Durant to lecture on the "History of Philosophy," response was so great that hundreds of people had to be turned away. Much to the delight of eager Seattle audiences, the Girls' Club was able to schedule the eloquent speaker for a return engagement of two evening lectures the next fall.

Because the Monday night club was so successful, the Women's Association with Mrs. Oren soon instituted a similar program for young married women on Thursday evenings. For

Sewing and fancy handwork were among skills taught at the Girls' Club.

women who worked in factories, they organized a Wednesday evening Industrial Girls' Club. For mature married women, they created the nondenominational Plymouth Institute for Women.

In 1926, the congregation purchased a three-story brick building at the corner of Sixth Avenue and Seneca Street adjacent to the church. The Women's Association transformed the former Engineers Club structure into Plymouth House, a boarding home for young women. The building had 22 bedrooms, a dining room, an auditorium, a large reception area, and club rooms for several other Seattle women's organizations, among them the Woman's City Club and Seattle Business and Professional Women. During the ensuing Great Depression, the building proved to be a financial albatross, strangling the church with maintenance and management expenses that far outweighed income. In 1936, trustees decided to tear it down and make way for a more lucrative parking lot.

One of the purposes of the Girls' Club was to provide community service. To this end members took responsibility for 10 high-school and grade-school groups of Camp Fire Girls, Girl Scouts, and Girl Reserves. In addition to a wide range of classes, members of these groups received dramatic coaching from Mrs. Sandall. Their performances on "Mothers' Night" and "Dads' Night" always received rave reviews. Because of Plymouth's program, these three major organizations for girls established a collaborative network through an all-city council of high-school girls.

Members of the Girls' Club and their youth organizations also enjoyed the fun of summer camp and winter outings in the snow with numerous opportunities for such sports as hiking, swimming, skiing, and tobogganing. Sometimes the different age groups had joint outings with the Young Men's or Boys' Club.

Plymouth member Paul Mason wrote an account of a 1920s trip to Mt. Rainier "when Longmire was as far as you could drive. There were about 125 of us (men and women) and we stayed at Elliott's camp just outside the park. We used the large building for eating and dancing and singing with Charlie (Anderson) playing the piano, and some of the other cabins for sleeping as well. Snow (was) on the road all the way from Longmire to the snout of the glacier. . . . Some hiked up to Eagle Peak as far as they could go, and some looked for the gold mine that was supposed to be on the way to the glacier."

Like Dr. Hawkins, his successor, Dr. Fifield, extolled the program, writing in the *Plymouth Girls' Club Annual* of 1928:

> I shall never forget the first visual impression of Plymouth Girls' Club. . . . The obvious spirit of friendliness evidenced in every part of the program, around the tables, the conversation, even the movement of the dishes across the tables toward the kitchen with a maximum of speed and a minimum of breakage, showed real team work and good will. I liked the songs and the way the songs were sung, and more than anything else, the intangible spirit and atmosphere that seemed to pervade the entire room. To me it seemed the sort of thing that Christ would want the church to be doing. Singing and golf, china painting, book reviews and all the rest, carried on in the proper spirit and atmosphere are essentially Christian in their expression.
>
> I have always been interested in the institutional program of the churches but had only known it in books and magazines. Now I know it at first hand, and I am constantly thrilled and inspired by the power and possibilities of it.

In 1935 after 14 years of existence, the Girls' Club that had played a vital part in so many lives was disbanded. The Rayner history records Miss Jorgensen's explanation: "When the Girls' Club was started there was no other organization in the city which was offering the program planned for the Club. There was a need for it. Plymouth responded and pioneered in this field. During the following years, other organizations and churches, realizing the value of such institutional work, developed similar clubs. And so it was that, with a decline in membership and the church facing financial problems, a combination of unfortunate circumstances, it was decided to discontinue the club . . ."

For Seattle girls and women, the closing of the Plymouth Girls' Club marked the end of a cherished era when for a few years they had had a unifying, harmonious, social and cultural center. In the early teens the YWCA had been a focus for working women, and in the late teens everyone was involved in the war effort. In the twenties, the Women's Association at Plymouth had grasped the opportune moment for a downtown organization. By the thirties, other such clubs emerged to draw members and, by the forties, another war brought an explosive population boom and consequent decentralization into suburban neighborhoods.

Beginning of the Fifield Years

By the time Dr. Hawkins resigned in May 1927 to accept a call to the First Congregational Church in San Francisco, he was widely acknowledged for leadership in the denomination and for his impressive accomplishments at Plymouth. During his six-year pastorate, he had substantially altered the theological and institutional priorities of the church. But as the trustees well knew, their dynamic leader had long had a metaphorical hole in his pocket in terms of the budget. Instead of diminishing, the lingering debt from the 1911 mortgage had increased.

The congregation culminated its search for a new pastor by calling the Reverend Dr. L. Wendell Fifield of Sioux Falls, South Dakota. He was a theologically liberal minister with a

The Reverend Dr. L. Wendell Fifield, 1927–1941

more conservative attitude toward finance. The Seattle press praised him as a clergyman who, by ability and attractive personality, had already gained national stature within Congregationalism.

In a September 1927 issue of the *Herald*, the new minister outlined his plans for the church: "For the present the work of the church as now organized will continue. The institutional work, a work that is considered by denominational leaders as one of the most significant Congregational projects in America, will be pushed forward aggressively with every effort to relate it as closely as possible to all church activities. . . . As I open this pastorate I have one deepest hope . . . to make Plymouth synonymous with helpfulness in Seattle." He emphasized the importance of all of the interrelated components of the religious service, mentioning in particular his coordination with Arville Belstad who had recently begun his long and distinguished career as organist and choirmaster of the church.

Dr. Fifield made his debut in the Plymouth pulpit with the Sunday morning topic, "If Jesus Came Down From the Cross." He stressed that the inward spiritual growth of the congregation must be nurtured through religious services and that the outward manifestation of that spirit must be service to the community. His evening sermon was entitled "The Thrilling Search for Truth." In it he confirmed his theologically liberal position and revealed an approach that differed from that of Dr. Hawkins.

This difference focused on Dr. Fifield's intense regard for liturgical tradition. He consistently strove to balance it with modern scholarship and the search for truth. In one of his early sermons, he said:

> If churchgoers consider the various parts of a service merely as preliminaries to the sermon, then Protestants are facing a serious problem with regard to their religion. . . . Liberal Protestants will never make priests out of their ministers, nor will they discontinue their search for truth. But they can make the order of service more genuinely expressive and uplifting. . . . We are not a liturgical church, but we need not pass off the Roman, Anglican, Lutheran, and Eastern church worship as ritualistic rubbish. Worship, after all, is the most important activity of the church. It is possible that we Protestants may be losing something with our method. Above all, we must get back to Christ worship.

When Dr. Fifield arrived in Seattle, theological liberalism was no longer perceived as shocking or bordering on blasphemy. By balancing his modernistic theological position with a respect for tradition, he was able to mend the breach that had alienated Dr. Hawkins from his conservative colleagues in other downtown Protestant churches. The next year fundamentalist Dr. Mark Matthews of the First Presbyterian Church delivered the Thanksgiving "Unity" sermon from the Plymouth pulpit.

One of Dr. Fifield's initial undertakings at Plymouth was to study all aspects of the church and, simultaneously, to get to know the members. His study soon revealed the precarious state of Plymouth's finances, and as he called on the members, he began quietly to remedy the situation. At the annual meeting in January 1929, Treasurer William S. Gruger happily reported that, for the first time in years, current bills were paid.

With the unqualified support of the trustees, Dr. Fifield now set out to eradicate the lingering $100,000 construction debt that was costing an annual $8,000 in interest. In early 1929, money seemed to flow freely as citizens stretched their investments and borrowing to the maximum, determined to realize the fabled American dream. The moment was ripe for Dr. Fifield to make his appeal. Of the $108,000 total, Roy Ballard, director of the fund-raising drive, credited the minister with personally obtaining pledges of $91,000. In a spring issue of the *Herald,* Mr. Ballard wrote: "We have never before had a pastor who has given so much support to the trustees, as Dr. Fifield. In his first year he balanced the current budget. In his second year he has razed the debt. This is the most important achievement in the history of Plymouth!"

According to various reports, the one-month campaign was carried out in such a manner that the majority of church members knew nothing about it. Relieved of the burden of debt, the congregation rejoiced. In the *Herald* article, Mr. Ballard quoted Dr. Fifield's salvo from the celebration banquet: "Now that we have the dollar sign out of our heads, we can work for the things that are really the goal of every church."

5
Sustenance in Hard Times 1930–1940

Heedless of gathering political storm clouds in Asia and Europe and largely oblivious to foreshadows of recession, Seattle neared the end of the twenties "stylish and stepping," revelling in the "jazz and ritz and bang and zip" of trendy Lake Washington Boulevard.[1] Instead of focusing on the changing times, many good citizens continued to trumpet the issue of prohibition, hurling hackneyed rhetoric at speakeasies, flappers, and bootleggers.

With the collapse of the stock market on the now-legendary "Black Tuesday" in October of 1929, the Roaring Twenties ground to a halt. In Seattle carefreeness and complacency gave way to foreboding and concern. The Plymouth congregation found new energy, nonetheless, for ecumenical and educational work that would see the church through the hard times of the Great Depression.

Like the cold, damp fog of winter, the depression enveloped and penetrated the city, rendering thousands out of work and homeless. Widespread despair permeated the downtown area. "Hooverville," a makeshift village of cardboard shacks, was home to otherwise-homeless men. It sprawled dismally along the tide flats just west of where the Kingdome now stands. Other homeless people sought shelter in abandoned downtown buildings.

Among the membership of Plymouth were many who were unable to honor their pledges. The fund-raising drive to retire the church's debt had begun early enough, however, so that by the fall of 1929, more than $30,000 in payments had been received. Although debt-free status would remain elusive for

1. Norma Rockliffe, *Argus Magazine*, Dec. 13, 1924.

years, Plymouth's financial picture was brighter than that of many other churches, all of which struggled to balance budgets in the face of substantially reduced donations.

In this decade prior to the advent of government social-welfare programs, the primary resources for the poor were churches and other community-service organizations. Under the leadership of Ward Bowman, Plymouth acted quickly to organize a relief department. Members and friends of the congregation were urged to contribute blankets, clothing, and food and to offer as many jobs as possible through an employment bank. Plymouth itself created employment opportunities for a number of workers by undertaking the first extensive renovation of its 20-year-old building.

Congregational and Christian Merger

Repairs and redecorating were timely, not only because of the age of the structure but also because Plymouth was expecting guests. The National Council of Congregational and Christian Churches had accepted Plymouth's invitation to host its historic meeting of 1931 at which the Congregational Church and the General Convention of Christian Churches would conclude and celebrate their merger.

All church departments contributed to the remodeling fund. The total budget was approximately $7,000, a sum that included a donation of $3,500 by the Women's Association to replace carpeting on the main floor and refurbish third-floor rooms. A renovation committee headed by W. L. Robbins coordinated the work and bolstered everyone's enthusiasm for the project. Even the boys' afternoon school contributed $25, no small feat for underprivileged lads whose economic lot had worsened considerably in recent times.

When the remodeling was completed, the congregation enthusiastically welcomed a record number of convention delegates who met from June 25 through July 5. Other Seattle Congregational churches joined in to help accommodate the visitors.

For the many delegates who considered anything Oriental to be exotic, the greeting extended by Seattle's Japanese Con-

Plymouth's ivy is in full leaf for this photo taken in the early 1930s.

gregational Church, complete with Nisei girls and women in ethnic dress, was a convention highlight. Because this occasion was only the third time that the Council had met west of Omaha since the Civil War, most of the visitors were new to the Pacific Northwest. In the best tradition of western hospitality, Clara Eckart as president of the Women's Association had carefully orchestrated details of hostessing, and the women of Plymouth were well-prepared to make their guests feel at home.

Delegates from the Congregational and Christian denominations met in separate sessions at which they reviewed the proposed constitution. After exchanging and approving suggested amendments, each body adopted the constitution, whereupon everyone marched from their meeting places and entered Plymouth's center doors in two columns to form a united body.

Congregational and Christian luminaries from Chicago Theological Seminary, Mills College, and even faraway Africa addressed the convention. On Friday evening a capacity audience filled Seattle's new Civic Auditorium for a public lecture.[2] The two floors of the auditorium were again taxed to the limit on Saturday evening when the men and women had their traditional separate banquets.

Two resolutions adopted at the close of the Council acknowledged the delegates' appreciation for what was commonly called "the best Council we have had." They read in part: "We have been blessed through coming in contact with the vigorous religious life of the Northwest and the Pacific slope . . . to Plymouth Church and to all the cooperating churches of Seattle and vicinity; to Dr. Fifield, notable for his sagacity, tireless graciousness and immensity of heart, and to all his like-spirited fellow workers, . . . we wish to voice our thanks, and with them leave God's blessing."[3]

Focus on Ecumenism

One of the primary emphases of the General Council was that "Christians must achieve unity." Writing in 1938 for the *Herald*, Dr. Fifield reflected that "ecumenical" was the "significant word of the decade." He emphasized the need to teach children that "the body of Christ's church is essentially one, that its purpose and its field are universal."

To this end Plymouth was especially active in the interdenominational Christian Endeavor movement. As a leader in the Washington-North Idaho Council of Churches and Christian Education, Plymouth in 1935 hosted 500 young people for a memorable three-day conference.

From the time that its building was erected in 1912, Plymouth had maintained office and library space for the Congregational Conference of Washington. At the beginning of the Great Depression, Seattle's former mayor, Bertha Landes, became the first woman to be Conference moderator. The times were particularly difficult for the Conference because it had to sustain smaller churches, especially those in rural

2. In the early sixties when Seattle prepared for the world's fair, the Civic Auditorium was gutted and refurbished as the present Seattle Opera House.

3. Alice E. Rayner, *The Path We Came By: A History of Plymouth Congregational Church* (Seattle, 1937), 142.

areas. As a consequence, it at one point had to drop support for its own minister. Conference leadership fell temporarily to the pastor in residence, namely Dr. Fifield. The offices remained at Plymouth until 1940 when the Conference was able to move into rented space.

In addition to cooperative work within the Conference, Plymouth participated during this decade in the Seattle Congregational Church Extension Society. It was a lay organization comprising elected delegates from all of the city's Congregational churches.

The simple, uncomplicated cooperation of downtown churches that began with Francis Van Horn had disintegrated with Chauncey Hawkins in the face of theological controversy. With Wendell Fifield the spirit of ecumenical cooperation revived and matured. Seemingly antithetical factions of the Protestant religious community began to get together to try to identify working relationships and philosophical points of agreement.

In 1940, Plymouth member Claude Eckart was president of the interdenominational Seattle Council of Churches that hosted a three-week evangelistic campaign featuring the dynamic Gypsy Smith, a popular evangelist of the time. Unlike most other Seattle churches, Plymouth chose to conduct regular Sunday and Wednesday evening services, rather than alter its schedule to accommodate the evangelist. Dr. Fifield explained: "I have a very deep admiration for Gypsy Smith. I realize that many can be reached by the methods of mass evangelism who can be reached in no other way. Personally, however, I cannot conscientiously cooperate in these meetings. I do not find any reality in this method of building the kingdom. Most of the leaders of our denomination share this conviction with me."[4]

Always the diplomat, Dr. Fifield had carefully outlined his position to members of the Council, and in return he, Mr. Eckart, and Plymouth were assured of the reciprocal spirit of

4. "Notes From Church Calendar," Feb. 1940. This commentary in the Plymouth archives is from bulletins published during the depression. From 1933 to 1937, the *Herald* was discontinued during summer months and after that time was published monthly. "J.F.H." who painstakingly compiled this commentary at times provided initialed margin notes.

goodwill. Acknowledging Gypsy Smith as "one of the great spiritual characters of our time" Dr. Fifield enticed him to preach a Sunday morning sermon from the Plymouth pulpit "in a service free from the usual evangelistic methods."

Tightening the Belt

At Plymouth the Great Depression forced a reevaluation of the church's extensive activities because the cost of operations was rapidly exceeding income. In 1932, staff members donated between 5 and 10 percent of their salaries to the budget. But in 1933, the trustees were forced to impose an additional 20-percent reduction in all wages. Some of the programs that the church had pioneered (such as the Girls' Club) were now being emulated by other nonprofit organizations and thus were discontinued. Pilgrim House, a center for students on the University of Washington campus, also had to be given up for lack of funds. Some signs of encouragement were evident, however. As chairman of the Benevolence Committee, Anson Burwell continued to solicit needed pledges, and members of the choir raised $500 for renovation of the organ.

With Lena Yuile as president, the Women's Association underwent a complete redistricting. It increased the number of circles from 8 to 15 and assigned every woman at Plymouth to a group in her neighborhood. The Young Married Women's Circle had luncheon meetings at the church, and business and professional women organized a downtown evening circle. Despite the demise of the Girls' Club, the women continued to sponsor Camp Fire, Girl Scouts, Girl Reserves, and Bluebirds.

For boys, the popular afternoon school continued, along with the George Colman Boys' Club and the Boy Scouts. Judge William G. Long was then presiding over the Seattle Juvenile Court. He frequently stated publicly that the program for boys at Plymouth Church had, in his estimation, reduced juvenile delinquency in the central downtown area by at least 50 percent. Successful businessmen, attorneys, physicians, laborers, and government workers were always present at Boys' Club reunions. These alumni and members of Plymouth's revitalized Men's Club were encouraged to become sustaining members of the Boys' Club.

During this belt-tightening period, Dr. Fifield introduced one new and innovative program to the church: the organization for young married couples that was Plymouth's first attempt at coeducation. Prior to this time, classes, fellowship groups, and even the boards of deacons and deaconesses had been segregated by sex. Young couples responded enthusiastically to the program that included a variety of social activities as well as Sunday morning religious education. This addition marked the beginning of further integration of men and women within the life of the church.

Outstanding Music

A spiritual oasis at Plymouth during the Great Depression and World War II was the outstanding music program capably directed by Arville Belstad. By 1937, membership in the Plymouth vested choir that sang on Sunday mornings had soared to the highest point in its history with a total of more than 70 voices. On Sunday evenings the Plymouth Motet Choir, a select group of 32 men and women, performed a more varied repertoire, including a cappella arrangements. On numerous occasions during the year, the Motet Choir gave special performances at Plymouth and throughout the region. Plymouth member Gene Daughters was in that choir and recalls that the group once dropped in on the governor, who graciously welcomed the choir for an impromptu private concert.

By the late thirties the Motet Choir had gained widespread popularity in the community. However, its origins a few years earlier had been anything but harmonious. Perhaps because they wanted a change, members of the congregation and choir had arranged to disband the locally renowned Plymouth Quartet, replacing it with the larger vocal ensemble. This move initially caused a cacophonous response; but in time, long-term quartet members and professional musicians Margaret Moss Hemion and James Harvey rededicated their talents to Plymouth's exemplary music program.

One of Mr. Belstad's most ambitious projects was creation of the Congregational Choral Union, a city-wide organization that also included the First Congregational Church of Everett. With approximately 150 voices, the massed choir for many years gave its annual concert at different Congregational churches and also appeared at Conference and ecumenical events.

Several other special music programs were offered at Plymouth, including the annual performance of Handel's *Messiah* that was broadcast over radio as "Plymouth's Christmas present to Seattle and the Northwest." In the spirit of the institutional church, Mr. Belstad also extended his ministry of music into the community. He directed the Seattle Orpheon (a prominent women's choral ensemble) and the equally notable Junior Amphion Society of 60 male voices.

In 1939, the church established an annual music festival featuring the music of Roman Catholic, Jewish, Russian Orthodox, and Protestant faiths. Festival music ranged from Negro spirituals to Mendelssohn's great *Elijah* oratorio and included sacred music from opera.

Prior to Mr. Belstad's retirement in 1943, Plymouth's choir performed on national radio and distinguished itself within the denomination for fund-raising. As gifts to Plymouth, it purchased a concert Chickering grand piano and an echo organ that could be played separately from the chapel in the back of the church or from the main organ console in the front. Mr. Daughters reports that "the musical effects with an echo organ and echo choir alternating with the main organ and full choir were often celestial in effect." Referring to the choir during these troubled times, notes in the archives state, "Music washes away from the soul the dust of everyday life."

The Popular Book Reviews

For each of the first 10 years of the Fifield pastorate, Plymouth ranked among the fastest-growing churches in the denomination. By 1940, membership totalled 2,099, with more than 1,000 scholars, teachers, and supervisors in the Sunday school. Contributing to the attraction were the foresight and personality of the senior minister himself. In an effort to build a strong Sunday evening service, he pioneered the almost instantly popular "book sermon," a review of a literary work from a theological perspective. With radio broadcasts of Sunday morning and evening services, Dr. Fifield reached a sizable extended audience.

His evening reviews featured such works as Pearl Buck's *The Patriot*, Rudyard Kipling's autobiography *Something of Myself*, Archie Binns' *The Land Is Bright*, Clarence Day's *Life With Father*, and Aldous Huxley's *Ends and Means*. On Sunday nights newcomers and members packed the house and, following the book review, remained to mingle over coffee. Many 50-year members of today's congregation recall a Fifield book review as their introduction to Plymouth.

Describing his extensive preparation, Dr. Fifield wrote: "I found it necessary to become conversant on the entire realm of literature. Especially interesting to me was the vast literature from the realm of science, repudiating the mechanistic theories and material philosophy of the nineteenth century and pointing the way to a new interpretation of spiritual reality. I found in modern fiction the story of the collapse of life without spiritual power and the development of life with it. A new consciousness of the immense amount of searching after truth that is characteristic of the world of today . . . came to me . . ."[5]

In 1937, Whitman College conferred on Dr. Fifield the honorary degree of Doctor of Letters. Archive notes proclaim it "an honor outstanding as coming from an institution of nationally recognized high scholarship; outstanding in that honorary degrees from Whitman College are sparingly granted after most careful investigation and also outstanding in the fact that the degree recognizes that eminence in the literary field was granted to a man in the field of ministry."

In addition to his programs at Plymouth, Dr. Fifield extended his ministry into the community by accepting numerous invitations as guest lecturer. Virginia Boren of *The Seattle Times* saw him as an almost-ideal composite of actor

5. The Reverend Dr. L. Wendell Fifield, "Four Symbolic Words: A Spiritual Autobiography," *Advance* (Sept. 6, 1934).

and minister, able to hold his audience "spellbound and breathless." In a 1937 article she described him as having "a fine choice of words; a flair for magnificent metaphors; a well-developed literary evaluation; a sense of humor; a sympathetic philosophy of people and life; a grand speaking voice; (and) a deep sense of the dramatic." Of the characters in his books, she said that Dr. Fifield made them come alive: "They seem to step out on the stage, act out their parts, and take their curtain calls."

Sunday Night Youth Program

In 1935, the book-review program at Plymouth was rescheduled for Wednesday evenings and broadcast over radio station KIRO's popular "It's a Case of Books." On Sunday evenings the church hosted the new nondenominational and largely nonsectarian program for youth co-sponsored by the city-wide Leisure Committee for Young People. It had the endorsement of civic leaders, among them Mayor Charles L. Smith.

The project was an innovation that, as far as Dr. Fifield knew, had never been attempted anywhere else. By bringing together community leaders and the city's leading advocates for youth, it was designed to offer a constructive social, religious, and recreational evening that would contribute to the young people's moral and spiritual development. The *Seattle Post-Intelligencer* that year quoted the minister as saying, "The young men or women who do not care to dance or spend the evening in a parked automobile on a lonely road can enjoy each others' company in the church."

Beginning at 6:30 P.M., the three-fold program offered young participants a choice of nine discussion groups led by civic, business, and educational leaders. An hour later Dr. Fifield presented a book review oriented to young people. Afterwards, everyone came together for an hour of singing, recreation, and refreshments, the latter provided by the Women's Association.

When the program entered its second year, it was under the sole sponsorship of Plymouth. Many of the young people had at first come because they had no other place to go. Now they evidenced a marked interest in a variety of church programs, which allowed Plymouth to project a more religious orientation.

In an effort to relate directly to problems facing youth, Dr. Fifield abandoned the original book-review format and instead invited young people to submit their requests for discussion topics. From the "Question Box" in the church, he selected four or five subjects a week, announcing them in the *Herald* so that participants could think about them in preparation for the next Sunday's discussion. Dr. Fifield wrote that fall in the *Herald* that he felt his method would contribute "vitally, practically, and pointedly to straight, clear Christian thinking in these important times." He appealed to the congregation: "I am anticipating the loyal cooperation of all Plymouth members and friends in making these Sunday evening services a tremendous religious power in Seattle."

As a follow-up to the "Question Box," Veo Small tapped his experience as Lakeside School administrator to organize a group for high-school and junior-college-aged youth, another for college and young business people, a current-events discussion group, a self-help session to explore personal problems, a drama department, and special classes in choral music, travel, science, art, and motion pictures. Like the George Colman Boys' Club, the program attracted a city-wide following, including large numbers of young people who lived downtown.

Personal Ministry

Despite his extensive public appeal and Plymouth's explosive growth, Dr. Fifield managed to maintain a deeply personal commitment to his parishioners, even to those who listened to his radio broadcasts. On many occasions he was called to the bedside of an unchurched listener to give comfort and guidance.

In the depths of the Great Depression, a couple named Slyfield had become acquainted with Plymouth via these broadcasts. Following her husband's death, Mrs. Slyfield sent for the pastor whom she knew only by his deep, resonant voice.

On a later Sunday when Dr. Fifield talked of the church's serious financial straits, she was listening. She called him and offered a donation of $5,000 to clear the immediate outstanding indebtedness. Following her death the next year, Plymouth became the beneficiary of a $25,000 endowment from the Slyfield estate, designated specifically for support of the radio program.

Like the Slyfields, many faithful listeners became friends of the church, sometimes making unsolicited contributions and at other times calling on the minister to conduct funerals, weddings, and baptisms or to counsel in times of crisis. Balancing his commitment to leadership and public education, Dr. Fifield urged his parishioners to share their thoughts with him and frequently reminded them that he was there as a counselor and friend. His bold-type exhortation in a fall 1939 issue of the *Herald* read: "DO NOT HESITATE TO CALL ME BECAUSE YOU THINK I AM TOO BUSY. I am anxious to be helpful in as many ways as I can these trying days. . . . Let's talk it over."

In early 1935, Dr. Fifield shared a personal tragedy with his congregation when, following a brief illness, his 43-year-old wife, Juanita, suddenly died. She had matched her husband's dedication and vigor in both the community and church, particularly in her work with the Women's Association. Members of the bereaved congregation contributed a set of chimes that later that year was dedicated in her memory.

A Deepening Sense of Heritage

During this period, members of Plymouth seem to have developed a deepening sense of their own heritage. Part of it was undoubtedly because of the troubled times that inevitably lead people to reflection. But an equally significant reason was the death of several cherished members who had helped weave the warp and weft of Plymouth and Seattle. The legacy shared by many children, grandchildren, and great-grandchildren drew the extended church family closer together.

Gone now were Judge Everett Smith and his wife Mary Dibble Smith, Leilla Shorey Kilbourne, Adelaide Lowry Pollock, Anson Burwell, Charles Horton, William Gruger, George and Laurence Colman, and their parents, James and Agnes. Although Laurence and the senior Colmans had transferred their membership to the Fauntleroy Church in their neighborhood, they had always maintained close ties to the downtown church. The passing of each of these people was felt by Plymouth and the city.

A year before she was killed in an automobile accident, Alice Rayner in 1937 captured the essence of the nostalgic feeling that swept the congregation: "There are only a few left now who can look back in memory upon the entire Plymouth scene. They were children in the days when Plymouth households managed without their dining tables while the Ladies' Aid was giving a bazaar or chicken dinner. . . . For no one else can Plymouth ever have quite the same meaning that it has for them. And when they go to join the church triumphant, something will go with them that can never be replaced . . ." What remained for the living were precedents established by many early members for lives of service.

Plymouth's anniversary celebrations during this period were indeed special. When the church observed its 70th anniversary early in 1940, lay members joined returning clergy to pay tribute to Congregational pioneers in the city. The Women's Association hosted a tea at which guests came dressed in costumes typical of those worn by Seattle pioneers. Governor Clarence Martin and Mayor Arthur B. Langlie were honored guests at the anniversary dinner at which they extended greetings from the state and city.

Reflections coupled with a bequest from the estate of Mrs. Kilbourne sparked renewed interest in an almost-forgotten plan. When the church was built in 1912, members intended to replace the sanctuary's plain windows with painted glass depicting the history of Congregationalism in the United States prior to the founding of Plymouth. The sanctuary was to be modeled after Brooklyn's historic Plymouth Church of the Pilgrims, revealing God's spirit in the context of modern events.

Payne-Spiers Studios of New York designed 11 windows, one of which was installed when the church was built. Located above the choir, the "Landing of the Pilgrims" was dedicated to John D. and Margaret Smith and portrays Governor

The "Landing of the Pilgrims" window above the choir was installed when the original building on Sixth Avenue was constructed. It is one of three that graced the sanctuary during this worship service in the mid 1960s.

Brewster, Governor Carver, and Priscilla Alden representing the Church, the civil government, and the family, respectively, with the Mayflower in the background.

Plans for the additional windows remained dormant for more than a quarter of a century, primarily because of the mounting deficit. They were to depict John Robinson's leading of the Pilgrims in their last prayer aboard the Speedwell, Pilgrims and Indians celebrating their first Thanksgiving, the historic 1806 Haystack Meeting at which American Congregationalists committed to support foreign missions, Manasseh Cutler's introducing of Protestantism to the West, Sacajawea with Lewis and Clark, Marcus and Narcissa

Dr. Edward C. Kilbourne demonstrates a woodworking technique for boys learning how to use equipment in Plymouth's manual-training shop.

Whitman at their mission near Walla Walla, the Denny party's landing at Alki, and the first Plymouth building in Seattle.

In the late 1930s, Mrs. Kilbourne left a bequest to create the "Old University of Washington" window in memory of her parents, Oliver C. and Mary E. Shorey. In honor of his deceased wife, Dr. Kilbourne funded the a second window: "Signing of the Mayflower Compact." These and the window from above the choir are preserved in the current structure.

Dr. Kilbourne's tribute was illustrative of his dedication to Plymouth that dated from the earliest days of the church. He taught for many years in the Sunday school and then ushered until the end of his life. He took his religion seriously but is also remembered for his sense of humor. Dressed in striped trousers, cutaway coat, black vest, wing collar, and, occasionally, a bright yellow tie emblazoned with a hula dancer, he usually chose to usher young women, especially blondes.

No one present could forget the 1955 summer camp at Seabeck when, at age 99, Dr. Kilbourne plunged off the diving board and waited until everyone was in a panic before popping up, laughing, 60 feet away. In honor of his birthday, Plymouth friends prepared a large cake that he proceeded to cut into very small pieces for the crowd assembled at camp, saying that he would take the remaining half back to share with "the boys on my floor at the 'Y'!" He contributed a lifetime of service to the YMCA, was a long-term leader in the Municipal League and Chamber of Commerce, and was a mainstay in the George Colman Boys' Club from its inception.

A Five-Year Plan

As they had grieved with Dr. Fifield over the loss of his wife, members rejoiced with him in the summer of 1936 when he married June Hayward. She had capably managed Plymouth's office during the long illness of church secretary Gertrude Evans. Following their wedding, the Fifields took a four-month vacation, and Dr. Francis Van Horn returned to his former parish to serve in their absence. While away from Seattle, Dr. Fifield reevaluated his program and on his return presented the members with his "Five-Year Plan" for aggressive forward movement by the church.

Among objectives stated that fall in the *Herald* were "study and revision of our entire educational program; readjustment of salaries, reduced during the depression, to insure permanence on the part of pastor and staff; addition of a minimum of 200 members each year with a goal of 2,500 active members by 1942; creation and development of a department of drama; and a deepening spiritual experience in our membership, and stronger spiritual leadership in Seattle."

By now the tide of the Great Depression had ebbed. More people were working, and ample signs of economic recovery were apparent. People also had a heightened awareness of Adolf Hitler as a serious threat to all of Europe and of the pressing need for a strong church.

The congregation responded wholeheartedly when Dr. Fifield voiced his concern for the whirlpool pattern of Plymouth's finances, a result of unpaid pledges carried over from the entire depression period. Consequently, final payments on each year's bills were being made from first receipts of the new year. The practice had been considered necessary as a stopgap measure to allow Plymouth to maintain its ambitious institutional and religious programs without increasing the existing debt. Dr. Fifield believed, however, that the policy could not be continued.

The kickoff of his five-year plan was a special Christmas offering that met the objective of collecting $5,000 to take care of the entire depression-era shrinkage. With increased income the trustees wisely made Plymouth one of the first churches in the country to establish the position of church business manager.

Claude Eckart accepted the appointment late in 1936. Parishioners read in their order of service this description of his qualifications: "He is preeminently fitted for this responsible position. He has served Plymouth Church in almost every volunteer capacity. He probably knows more Plymouth members personally than any other member of our church. . . . As Chairman of the Board of Trustees the past years, his service has been notable, and he has secured a full knowledge of the business side of our work."

In all of Plymouth's programs, Dr. Fifield's focus on increased spirituality reigned. Deacons worked in neighborhoods throughout the city to organize fellowship groups. With Ward Bowman's leadership, the graded Sunday school sought to strengthen all of its programs, bringing in the latest and best study materials. The Young People's Class explored the origin and content of the New Testament with Edward Lauer, dean of the College of Arts and Sciences at the University of Washington. Professor Edward Wagenknecht from the University's English Department led the Young Married People's Class, helping them interpret the Bible in light of modern scholarship. Still another University professor, Linden A. Mander of the Political Science Department, facilitated the Adult Group's discussion of the world's contemporary social and religious conditions.

The drama program was also meeting with success. For the first time in its history, the Seattle Repertory Playhouse in 1936 allowed a group other than the Repertory Players to mount plays on its stage. That group was Plymouth's Young People's Dramatic Club directed by John W. Solomon. In widely publicized presentations of three one-act plays, the troupe furthered the relationship between church and drama.

Explaining the unique program at Plymouth, Dr. Fifield wrote in the fall of 1937:

> Plymouth Church is nationally recognized as one of the outstanding institutional churches of the United States. . . . I am confident that our type of organization most nearly expresses the attitude of the spirit of Jesus. . . . The book reviews are attracting large numbers of young people. . . . Plymouth Church has the fifth largest Church school in the Congregational denomination. In every department the purpose is very definitely to teach nothing now that must be unlearned later. . . . It is this institutional program which has led many influential citizens of Seattle who are not members of Plymouth Church to make the statement that Plymouth is the most important single religious institution in the city. This statement has frequently been corroborated by ministers of denominations other than our own.

The International Forum

From the beginning of his pastorate, Dr. Fifield had viewed the increasingly turbulent international situation with deep sensitivity, as evidenced in his book-review and sermon topics. A spring 1934 notice in Seattle's *Jewish Transcript* announced: "Distinguished champion of good-will between Jews and Christians, the Reverend Dr. L. Wendell Fifield, pastor of Plymouth Congregational Church, will review Hitler's autobiography, *Mein Kampf*, this evening at Herzl Synagogue Conservative services, and interpret it as a key to the character of the man responsible for the greatest persecution of Jewry in modern times."

At Plymouth the sermons in 1938 included a trilogy entitled "Christ and Stalin—Love vs. Fear," "Christ and Mussolini—Love vs. Force," and "Christ and Hitler—Love vs. Hate." In late 1939, the *Herald* reported that a survey of radio listeners had revealed that "Plymouth Church was making a real contribution to the cause of peace." As the situation in Europe worsened, Dr. Fifield combined his "Question Box" and book-sermon formats to create a new Sunday evening "International Forum."

Describing its purpose in the *Herald* a few weeks later, he said: "Two things are necessary to keep America at peace: First, clear, honest, fearless thinking. Second, an outlet for the frank exchange of opinions to guard against emotional high tensions. Plymouth's unique leadership in Seattle gives it the opportunity to become the center for continuous, intelligent, reasoned discussions of the international situation. Thus we can make an outstanding contribution to the community and to the nation. We can help make America steady."

Seattle audiences rallied to the International Forum with an average attendance of 1,000. When Dr. Fifield reviewed *The Voice of Destruction— Hitler Speaks* by Herman Rauschning, the auditorium overflowed with 1,600 present. Among other forum topics were "A Second Look at *Mein Kampf* in the Light of Current Events," "The New World Menace of Russia," and "The Queer Case of Those Who Defend Russia and Denounce Germany."

As the possibility of America's participation in the war grew imminent, Dr. Fifield prepared his congregation. He began offering a series of Sunday morning sermons on spiritual values and personal religion and instituted a much-appreciated interdenominational Thursday morning "Quiet Hour" for women. A fall 1940 issue of the *Herald* called it "a period of spiritual refreshment, prayer, and instruction," promising that "every effort will be made to keep all of the material well within the scope of peace and quietness" and expressing the hope that it would prove to be "an oasis in the midst of the busy, turbulent times in which we are living."

While keeping his parishioners vigilant and informed about turbulent world events, Dr. Fifield simultaneously strove to keep them spiritually assured and strong within themselves so that they could deal with the times. Another issue of the *Herald* that fall provides an example of his consistent thesis that "the church is the only institution which still brings a message of hope rather than fear to the hearts of people." Hearing that message of hope would be imperative during the war years ahead.

6 War and Peace 1940–1950

By 1940, the national preparedness program had begun. For Seattle it would mean growth and prosperity. The city anticipated that the burgeoning shipping and airplane industries would lure thousands of new workers and their families. For Plymouth it meant the hard work of being a church amidst the trauma of another world war and the changes that were sure to come in its wake.

These were years of the Boeing boom. From 4,000 workers in 1939, the company mushroomed to more than 50,000 by 1944, taking its place as the dominant force in the local economy. Military bases also drew a huge influx of newcomers into the area.

Politics and Patriotism

Plymouth members seemed to have resigned themselves to the policy of conscription; at the same time they believed that the government should try every avenue for peace before resorting to war. When the military draft began in the fall of 1940, Plymouth invited young men and their families for a special service. Americans were still hoping that their country would remain neutral, and Dr. Fifield sought to reassure his congregation. As quoted in the *Seattle Post-Intelligencer*, he said: "While it is true that very few of those who register will actually be called for military training, the very fact of registering inevitably is bringing many serious thoughts to young men." He offered church programs and his personal counseling as resources that could be "helpful and useful in the readjustments, either in thinking or living, that may be created.'' With uncharacteristic equanimity, Dr. Fifield continued, ''The church cannot alter the fact that this registration is being made . . .'' He could not know that the coming hostilities would claim his son, Bob.

One avowed pacifist in the congregation was Professor Edward Wagenknecht who, in addition to his degree in English, had completed the necessary studies to become a Congregational minister. A devoted member of Plymouth, Dr. Wagenknecht had on occasion preached from the pulpit. However, because of the church's acceptance of the draft, he withdrew to become a Quaker.

If the draft issue was generally moot at Plymouth, other political questions were not. Frederica Mead Hiltner and her husband, Walter, had been missionaries in China. She was among members of the church who joined picket lines on the waterfront to protest shipment of scrap iron to Japan. In Washington State politics, many Plymouth people rallied to the support of Seattle Mayor Arthur B. Langlie in his bid for governor against King County Commissioner John C. Stevenson. In a *Herald* article published during the campaign, Dr. Fifield labeled Mr. Stevenson ''a would-be demagogue . . . a machine politician of the worst type.'' In addition to other objectionable activities, he was said to have solicited and received support from the Communist Party.

Following the general election, the minister used the *Herald* to praise his congregation: ''This is a good example of the church in politics. Moral issues were paramount. . . . Perhaps the greatest menace to good government in the history of the state was averted when (Stevenson) was defeated, and by so close a margin that the activities of Plymouth members, headed by Fred Baker, Langlie's campaign manager, may well have swung the balance against him.''[1] To succeed Mr. Langlie as mayor, many Plymouth people supported the victorious William F. Devin, who for the next 12 years gave the city what historians have evaluated as exemplary leadership.

All of Plymouth revelled in deserved pride when in late 1940 the Board of Realtors designated Dr. Fifield Seattle's First

1. John Stevenson lost in the primary election against C. C. Dill of Spokane who was later defeated by Langlie.

Citizen. The minister was the second recipient of the prestigious annual award; the first was Dr. Richard Fuller, founder and director of the Seattle Art Museum. As chairman of Plymouth's Board of Trustees, Kenneth Morford expressed the feelings of the congregation. He wrote in the *Herald:* "We can be proud not only because he is our pastor, but also because it is a recognition of the value to the community of the work being done at Plymouth."

As the nation girded itself for defense, a heightened spirit of patriotism began to envelop the land. Dr. Fifield became head of the Seattle Red Cross and in early 1941 made his "I Believe in the United States" address to the downtown Kiwanis Club. Classes in Seattle schools and in schools throughout the state were interrupted so that students could listen to a broadcast of the speech. The *Herald* reported that the speech received widespread acclaim as one of the most extensive attempts in education for good government ever carried through in Seattle.

For some time members had realized that their illustrious minister had captured national attention and admiration throughout the denomination. They were not greatly surprised, then, when in April 1941 Dr. Fifield reluctantly announced his decision to accept the call of the historic Plymouth Church of the Pilgrims in Brooklyn, New York. The attractive and challenging offer had been influenced by church leaders who envisioned the Brooklyn church once served by Henry Ward Beecher as the potential cathedral church of Congregationalism.

While saddened by Dr. Fifield's departure, the Seattle congregation gratefully recognized what his unprecedented 14-year pastorate had done for their church and the community. With a membership of nearly 2,000, one of the largest Sunday schools in the country, and an exemplary community-service program, Plymouth had made significant contributions to Protestantism and had garnered considerable national recognition. Dr. Francis Van Horn once again returned as interim pastor. In his words, his task was "to maintain the high level of these past splendid years."

In February of 1942 just after the bombing of Pearl Harbor, the Reverend Dr. Allan I. Lorimer and his wife, Mary, arrived

The Reverend Dr. Allan I. Lorimer, 1942–1946

from Manchester, New Hampshire. A caring, compassionate pastor, Dr. Lorimer did a commendable job of succeeding Dr. Fifield and of holding the downtown church together during the war years. Prior to gas rationing, he preached to some of the largest congregations ever assembled at Plymouth.

Also new to the staff in 1942 was Harold V. Smith. The son of Plymouth pioneers Judge Everett and Mary Dibble Smith, he would serve the church as executive secretary for almost 20 years. He brought with him a commitment fostered in his youth and deepened in his maturity. With wit and candor, he regaled younger generations with stories about his boyhood and at the same time reminded Plymouth people of their heritage and mission. During the war years, he helped Dr. Lorimer keep the church strong in order to nurture its members and serve the broader community.

The Japanese American Experience

While evicting Chinese laborers in the 1880s, the United States had been courting trade with Japan. As a consequence, Japanese began to immigrate to West Coast cities. By the turn of the century, they constituted Seattle's largest ethnic group. In 1941, Japanese Americans numbered 7,000 in the city of 350,000.

Restrictive immigration laws in the twenties had divided the Japanese American population into older Issei (first-generation immigrants who had arrived before the codes were imposed) and generations born in America. Encouraged by their elders to assimilate, the Nisei (second-generation) were by now taking their place in the schools, work force, and general social fabric of the community. Nonetheless, the majority of white people knew little about "Japantown" in the central part of the city where most Nisei lived and where the Issei retained their ethnic language and traditions.

Just days before Pearl Harbor, the *Herald* carried a notice about a basketball game featuring a Japanese American team from the George Colman Boys' Club and a team of Chinese American boys. Plymouth had several Japanese families among its members and in addition had enjoyed a long-standing, close relationship with Seattle's Japanese Congregational Church.

Three months after Pearl Harbor, life for Japanese Americans in Seattle changed dramatically. President Roosevelt signed Executive Order 9066 that instructed the military to evacuate anyone of Japanese descent from designated strategic areas, including coastal regions of the Western states.

Today, many remember the events that followed as some of the most disreputable in Seattle history. Despite the fact that no charges were ever filed against them, Japanese American men, women, and children were herded onto buses, taking with them only what they could carry. They were transported under military guard first to the stables on the Puyallup fairgrounds and then within a few weeks to "permanent" inland camps, mostly in Idaho. Some families arranged to leave property in the care of trusted friends. The rest were forced to sell possessions at far below their value or to abandon them altogether.

After the evacuation some members of the congregation kept in touch with friends in the internment camps. An order of service in mid 1942 quotes a letter from George Takagawa, former president of the George Colman Boys' Club, to his Christian education colleague Ward Bowman, saying: "Life here is not too hard, although we are deprived of many city conveniences. We are not being mistreated but neither are we being coddled. . . . Unfortunate though it may be considered, to me it is rather an adventure in witnessing the workings of a democracy in wartime in handling a portion of the population, which is in an ambiguous position, so to speak. We are well and not downhearted."

In that same order of service, a more critical Dr. Lorimer observed that "the Japanese who are American citizens have been interned not by due process of law but by presidential edict. It means that the President can send any group of us he wishes to internment camp. No hearing need be granted us. No right of defense. Only a signature is required. Therein lies the tragedy."

In January 1943, the International Forum featured a debate regarding the rights of Gordon Hirabayashi, an American awaiting trial in King County for refusing to be evacuated. Mary Farquharson of the American Civil Liberties Union argued that the evacuation policy came about largely because of propaganda not based on fact. Plymouth's Walter Hiltner took the side of President Roosevelt and the government. Mr. Hirabayashi's conviction that year was upheld by the U.S. Supreme Court; but in 1986 the court exonerated him. By association, his was a victory for all West Coast Japanese Americans who had been interned.

Following the war, evacuees returned home, wanting most of all to reestablish themselves in the community and ensure a better future for their children. True to their cultural heritage, they kept the hurt and humiliation primarily to themselves. In 1986, the Plymouth Forum featured excerpts from *Breaking the Silence,* a new play by Seattle's Nikki Lewis. This portrayal of the evacuation provided a cathartic experience for many of those who had lived in the camps and forced others finally to acknowledge the xenophobia and racism that had for decades generally gone unchallenged.

The Red Scare

People paid little heed to the internment of Japanese Americans during wartime. They could not, however, ignore vocal spokesmen of the American Communist Party who applauded this country's alliance with Stalinist Russia. In a letter to his sons in the summer of 1944, Harold Smith described what he called a "riot in the sanctuary": "The American Friends Service Committee (Quakers) are holding an Institute of International Relations here . . . with a number of nationally known speakers . . . with the first four evening sessions at Plymouth Church. . . . The Communist Party wrote a letter to the mayor protesting the meetings on the grounds that they were a 'Peace Now' movement and that some of the speakers were 'Trotskyites.' "

From Sunday through Wednesday evening, groups of Communists crashed the gate to heckle and interrupt the programs. During the first three evenings, speakers were able to prevail despite increasingly boisterous crowds. Anticipating a crisis at the final session, Mr. Smith arranged for Seattle police officers to be present but instructed them to take no action except on his orders.

With a crowd of 800 (a fourth of whom were radicals), the chairman tried in vain to appeal for free speech and fair play, promising everyone ample opportunity for response after the address. Public stenographers recorded all that was said and were able to get the names of several shouting, gesturing men who claimed to represent unions for such groups as longshoremen and machinists. When radicals seized the microphone, Mr. Smith cut off power, and the chairman closed the meeting. In his letter, Mr. Smith evaluated the event:

> It was a disgraceful exhibition of un-Americanism and the presence in our community of an active body of communists. In retrospect I know that I acted wisely. The prestige of the church has been enhanced for refusing to submit to bullying tactics. It would have resulted in bloodshed and

property damage if the police had tried to preserve order and eject the disturbers. The press (three large dailies) unanimously condemned those who made the demonstration, pointing out that they were the same tactics used by Hitler when he was coming into power. I feel that it was an eye-opening experience for the city. If labor has for its leadership the men who claimed to speak for some of their unions, there is little hope that our traditional American institutions can be preserved. Fortunately they are still a minority, but they indicate a bad situation. The police have been so criticized that I have told the chief I shall write to the editors and take responsibility for their failure to act.

Responding to Needs at Home

The entire community was in a state of heightened agitation after the U.S. declaration of war. Young men enlisted or were drafted into military service. Young women had numerous choices. Some volunteered for military duty or the Red Cross, and others joined "Rosie the Riveter" to do "men's work" and maintain the strength of the civilian labor force.

Plymouth also rallied to attempt to preserve basic values, to bolster faith and confidence, and to provide an island of sanity in a topsy-turvy world. Chaplains from Paine Field, Fort Lewis, and Fort Warden wrote to Dr. Lorimer expressing their appreciation for the Sunday night youth program and their desire to cooperate in making it known to "boys" in the service.

In an effort to meet changing needs, the Sunday school with Louise Triplett as its new director adjusted some of its programs. The young-adult and college groups in particular were reoriented to include military personnel. The Women's Association saw that soldiers attending Sunday services received a special welcome and an invitation to members' homes for dinner.

Dr. Lorimer recruited Marion Fish Cox to teach the college class that she reorganized to include "not only University students, but also white collar girls, Boeing riveters, assembly line workers, and soldiers, some of whom were regular, while

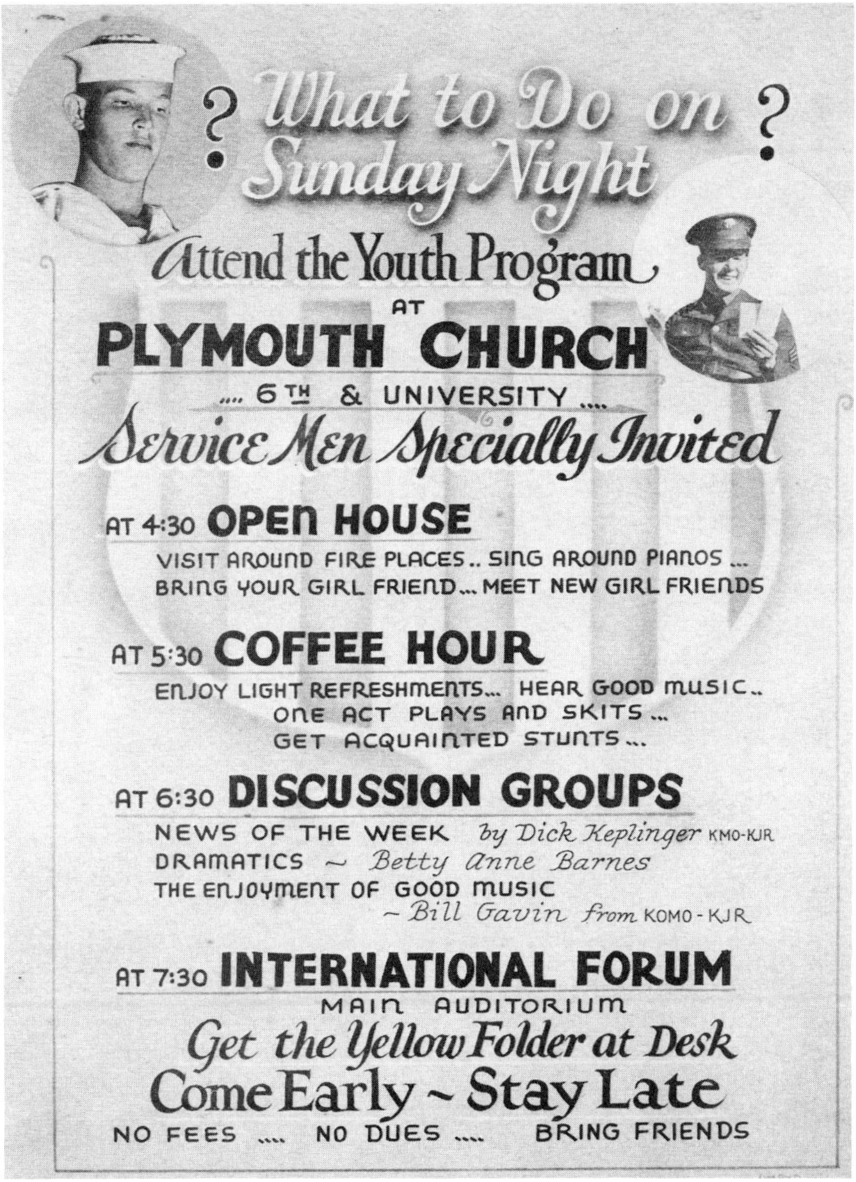

Plymouth attracted servicemen during World War II with this extensive program.

others were en route.'' Early on Sunday mornings Mrs. Cox and her husband Will (who was dean of the College of Business at the University of Washington) took alder logs to the church parlor and built a roaring fire in the huge fireplace. Warmed by the crackling blaze, the young people met for a discussion based on the theme "Faith in Living" and for singing around the piano, after which they attended the regular morning service. As an example of Plymouth's hospitality programs, the Coxes almost always asked a few of the young men and women to their home after church.

Seeking greater opportunity for fellowship, members of the college class organized a new group called the Plymyouthians. Dr. Lorimer was often present when the group met in private homes for informal chats or had holiday parties, picnics, and other outings. The church hosted Sunday luncheons in the dining room with GIs as guests. Circles took turns assisting Plymouth's cook and creating a warm, friendly atmosphere. These popular luncheons continued until 1954.

One of the programs that felt the impact of war most strongly was the Boys' Department. Many older boys enlisted in the armed services or worked seven days a week in defense plants. Dr. Lorimer urged all of the boys, especially members of the George Colman Boys' Club, to develop themselves spiritually, mentally, and physically. He emphasized the importance of carrying on normal activities, including the Thursday night hobby shop, Sunday afternoon school, summer camp, fall bean feed, and the Christmas dinner that was still furnished by the Colman family.

As in 1917, Plymouth again became a center for Red Cross work and first-aid training. The Women's Association organized several service groups. One brought together women to sew comfort bags, garments, and "housewives" (pouches that contained items such as needles, thread, soap, and safety pins) for the Red Cross to give to soldiers. Another group met three times a week to make surgical dressings, producing a grand total of 242,285 by the end of the war.

Women from the church also staffed the snack bar at the Service Men's Club on Fridays and were hostesses for the Army-Navy YMCA. On the fourth Sunday of every month, Plymouth women supplied and served refreshments for more than 1,000 military personnel at the United Service Organization (USO) that was sponsored by the Seattle Council of Churches. In addition to its usual charitable commitments to home and foreign missions, the Women's Association contributed substantially to overseas relief, sending used clothing, other supplies, and financial donations.

The *Herald* carried increasingly long columns naming the congregation's enlisted men and a few women, noting those who were killed in action. As groups of soldiers prepared to go overseas, Plymouth Rocks (the successor to the Men's Club) frequently entertained them. On their return, members of the group welcomed them home with informal dinners.

In an effort to maintain a semblance of continuity and stability, Dr. Lorimer wrote personal letters to every member of the congregation who went to war. One special Sunday evening service was a civic tribute to the war's unsung heroes: the men of the Merchant Marines. The 50-voice Sea-Tac Men's Chorus presented a concert of patriotic songs, including the international hymn of seafarers, "Eternal Father, Strong to Save."

A Debt-Free Church

Faced with an aging building and ever-increasing needs for benevolences, Plymouth continued to heed the fund-raising priorities established during the Fifield years. In the spring of 1943, Dr. Lorimer credited his predecessor and the congregation for their vigilance in trying to eliminate the debt that had lingered since 1911 when church construction began: "Fifteen years ago the debt was well over $100,000. Through the heroic effort and sacrifice of Dr. Fifield and the people of the church the total indebtedness has been reduced so that today it is approximately $6,000." On that Easter Sunday, 2,300 people attended services and contributed to a special offering.

In the next Sunday's order of service, the minister jubilantly proclaimed, "We shall burn the mortgage. Every cent of indebtedness at Plymouth has been cleared."

The achievement of the long-sought, debt-free status was a tremendous morale booster for the congregation. In a celebratory mood the members increased benevolences and also established a fund for a memorial chapel to be dedicated in honor of Plymouth's forthcoming 75th anniversary. The original plan was to build the chapel on the parking lot next to the church. A shortage of materials and other wartime priorities, however, required postponement of the project until 1949. As other remodeling plans developed, the trustees finally decided to integrate the chapel into the balcony area above the narthex. It became an intimate setting for numerous events, including small weddings, funerals, and private baptisms.

Harold Smith praised Plymouth for its "excellent financial condition." Following the end of the war in 1945, he wrote in his annual report, "We are thankful that we have been able not only to meet our operating expenses but also to contribute more generously than ever before to the world wide needs of the church and of humanity."

A Return to 'Normalcy'

Plymouth's concerted effort to maintain an island of normalcy during the war had left the congregation spiritually strong and loyal to its institutional and missionary program. The times had also taken their toll, however, and the need for revitalization was apparent. The *Herald* and radio broadcasts of Sunday services had been suspended as economy measures. The Sunday school program was stagnating, and the building needed repair.

By 1945, the church felt the effects of gasoline rationing. Suburban churches that Plymouth had helped to foster were drawing people who could not spare the gas to drive beyond their neighborhoods. Overtime and graveyard shifts in war industries and the absence of younger men gone to active service also exacted a price. Church attendance dropped to some 600 on Sunday mornings, and the Sunday evening forum faded. This downturn reflected national trends; congregations everywhere were trying to attract the distracted unchurched back into the fold.

In retrospect, Dr. Lorimer's 1945 annual report might be interpreted as almost congratulatory for himself and for Plymouth, rather than apologetic. He wrote: "We have hewed the line and held our own. We have made no spectacular advance in any area of the church, with the exception of finance. I believe we have kept faith with God and that increasingly our church is making more solid the rock of the Holy Spirit on which all churches should be built . . ."

Plymouth did, indeed, emerge from the war years in better shape than many other churches. Despite its problems, it was at long last free of debt and still had a comparatively large and devoted membership with a lay leadership that included many of the city's foremost citizens.

With the surrender of Japan came jubilant celebrating in the streets of Seattle. What everyone hoped for most of all was a return to normal life. Boeing adjusted to the peacetime economy, reducing its work force by 80 per cent. Among the first workers to be laid off there and elsewhere were women in nontraditional jobs. When Boeing began to hire again, the jobs were offered to war veterans.

The ideal home supported by a working husband and made comfortable and nurturing by a devoted wife and mother was an almost-universal dream. Marriages abounded, and cozy family neighborhoods blossomed in the suburbs. A notable contributor to the outward surge was Plymouth's Nathaniel Allen Carle, architect of the avante garde floating bridge that in 1939 opened Mercer Island and the east side of Lake Washington to rapid development. By the post-war years, the era of commuter traffic had arrived. For many suburbanites, getting to work or to the downtown church via the crowded bridge or Aurora Avenue North (Highway 99) was the greatest challenge of the day.

For churches, the time was ripe for recruiting new suburban families. With Phoebe Jared as president, the Women's Association in 1949 began a concerted effort to draw new homemakers into neighborhood circles. One of the major annual events was the autumn Plymouth Towne Faire. It brought the entire Women's Association together with circles from all parts of the greater metropolitan area participating. Members of each circle arranged a brightly decorated booth to display and sell their artwork, crafts, and homemade delicacies. A highlight of the event was always the colorful display by the Plymouth Quilters, a group of older needle artists

Members of the Women's Association put the finishing touches on the 1959 "Plymouth Towne Faire," a popular annual fund-raising event for missions.

who had weekly quilting bees at the church and kept alive this intricate folk art.

In addition to the displays, church musicians and drama groups shared their talents, and all enjoyed the abundance of tempting food. The Women's Association's cook planned lunch and dinner, along with an afternoon tea featuring hot scones. Long-time member Evelyn Gunther co-chaired the event one year with Helena Robbins and remembers with gratitude that "the whole city would come" in response to invitations from friends and associates at Plymouth.

Under the leadership of Major Walter T. Guthrie, the men's Plymouth Rocks also emerged from the war years with renewed dedication to all aspects of church work. The group designed a monthly program to attract both old and new members and vowed to cooperate with other Seattle churches in an interdenominational effort to restore religious activity to its prewar popularity. Plymouth men acted on a request from county commissioners by appointing Frank Moran to recruit an interfaith committee to build a prisoners' chapel in the county jail.

In December 1946, Dr. Lorimer resigned so that he and his wife could be with their daughter who was seriously ill in the East. On an interim basis, the Reverend Dr. R. Franklin Thompson from the University of Puget Sound conducted Sunday services and Wednesday dinner meetings.

Following Dr. Lorimer's departure, the Reverend Dr. Newton E. Moats of Seattle First Methodist wrote a tribute published in his church's newsletter: "Allan was my friend. I have never been closer to any minister . . . About once a week we would burn the midnight oil together, talking 'shop,' sharing our theological peculiarities AND RELIGIOUS CONVICTIONS. . . . On his insistance the downtown pastors met together occasionally for lunch, and there developed a spirit of fellowship that has drawn these downtown congregations closer together."

The men's group undertook publication of a short-lived church weekly, the *Plymouth News.* In the first issue, it announced the arrival of a new senior minister, the Reverend Dr. Dwight L. Cart from Faith Congregational Church in Springfield, Massachusetts. It outlined plans for welcoming him, his wife, Elsie, and their son to Seattle. In preparation the church purchased a house in Laurelhurst as its first parsonage.

When Dr. Cart stepped into the Plymouth pulpit on Mother's Day, 1947, he was welcomed by a congregation of 1,152. His ability to deliver sermons without notes made him a very popular, colloquial preacher.

Robert Sandall was chairman of the Board of Deacons at the time and wrote in his annual report: "The coming of Dr. Cart was like a tonic. . . . We had labored under the idea that we were badly handicapped, due to the fact that we were a downtown church. Dr. Cart emphatically denied this proposition. He pointed out, on the contrary, that we were in a tremendously strategic location."

For many it seemed as if Plymouth had gained two new

The Reverend Dr. Dwight L. Cart, 1947–1952

ministers. Like her husband, the eminently qualified Elsie Cart gave her full support to church and community work. In the city she was active in the YWCA, the Girl Scouts, the League of Women Voters, and the Women's University Club. The latter asked her to repeat her series of highly acclaimed book reviews, initially sponsored by the Women's Association of Plymouth.

The Colonies

One of the problems of downtown churches is that parishioners lack the close day-to-day contact with one another inherent in neighborhood congregations. Dr. Wendell Fifield and the deacons had tried to remedy the problem by forming neighborhood groups; but the minister's departure and the ensuing war had thwarted these efforts.

From its inception a colony plan showed greater promise. Key members from each neighborhood were chosen to be district governors and coordinate activities for Plymouth people who lived near them. In an article that brought national attention to this system and to Plymouth, Theresa Stevens wrote: "Because all activities are designed for family participation, husbands and wives work together. For this reason the office of chairman is called a 'governorship,' although the wife—when the position is held by a couple—usually is the more active worker because of the time she has to give and because of her position as hostess at home meetings."[2]

Plymouth's colonies were in tune with the post-war return to normalcy, the baby boom, and the emphasis on family life. Charles and Denny Burton, LeConie and Helen Stiles, Delia and Eleonora Bergstrom, and other members demonstrated that men and women could be equal partners in church leadership.

With Mrs. Stiles as the first governor-general, the church divided the community into 17 colonies, each of which had its own leaders. For a number of years ministers and their wives attended these colony meetings, availing themselves of an invaluable means of generating and promoting fresh ideas and of recruiting support in terms of both volunteer workers and financial donations to church programs.

In her article Mrs. Stevens wrote: "Every colony, like every neighborhood, has its own personality. No effort is made to create uniformity. The Christian spirit of fellowship directs all expression and purpose, but the mood of the meetings is always one of joyous sociability, of casual gayety, of more abundant living." While some of the colonies contributed to missionary work, others focused on local service programs. One chose to repair toys that the colony members then donated to welfare organizations. In each of the colonies a steering committee organized small dinners to include new members and to ensure "that every member will either be a

2. Theresa Stevens, "Plymouth Colony Goes West," *Advance*, (Jan. 7, 1952), 18–21.

Plymouth neighbors in northeast Seattle are enjoying this colony get-together.

guest of or a host to every other member.'' Colonies met in homes two or three times a year and came together for Thanksgiving dinner at the church.

Theresa and James Stevens frequently hosted their colony in Madrona. There and at all-church gatherings, the singing often included rousing choruses of ''The Frozen Logger Who Stirred His Coffee With His Thumb.'' This hit song by the Weavers came from the fertile imagination of Mr. Stevens who recorded the mighty feats of Paul Bunyan and was one of the first Pacific Northwest writers to achieve critical acclaim.

In reflections for the Plymouth archives, Phoebe Jared wrote that the neighborhood colonies ''created a resurgence of true sociability wherein individuals learned to know each other as human beings capable of deep friendship in both joy and sorrow. In some instances nonmember guests, who were always welcome at colony gatherings, found in them an answer to their search for a home church. As a result of these colonies, a warming, more personal friendliness was felt throughout the church.''

The success of the colonies generated enthusiasm for clubs designed to draw like-minded people together. The Tandem Club was organized in 1951 as a new group for young married couples. Robert and Virginia Hildebrand were its first co-presidents. During the same period, single young adults began to meet on Sunday evenings for Young Adults (later known as Fireside Fellowship). Under the leadership of Ruth Ittner, Lorraine Bennett Bristow, Bud Schoettler, and others, the fellowship met for such events as volleyball and table-tennis matches, biweekly square dances in the church dining room, and casual dinners. Along with their social activities, both groups had discussions about church programs and, like the colonies, contributed to their support. So many marriages resulted in the 1950s that Fireside Fellowship eventually fell victim to its own success.

Emphasis on Youth

One of Dr. Cart's most difficult hurdles in the late forties was an outmoded Sunday school program. A dedicated band of teachers included several who had served for more than 45 years. They confidently employed time-honored methods (mostly memorization) to teach sex-segregated classes and sometimes moved along with the same group of students for as many as 8 to 12 years.

The Reverend Robert Owen was minister of Christian education. He worked with his wife, Chris, with the Carts, and with innovative lay people to try to implement changes. Among them was adoption of approved Congregational curriculum materials. Mr. Owen also broke up the large, common Sunday school area by enclosing balcony space so that classes could be separated.

As head of the Christian Education Committee, Eva George later recalled the controversy over coeducational classes: "Many teachers . . . like Dr. Kilbourne and Miss (Jennie) Holbrook, for example, had been teaching for years and years the same way, and they didn't want to change. Dr. Kilbourne didn't think he could manage if he had a mixed class, and Miss Holbrook didn't want to teach boys; she just wanted to teach girls. I finally had to ask her to quit. The first year after they did combine seemed to work out all right. . . . I don't remember that we had any big difficulty."

Rejuvenation of the education program continued into the next decade. Following Mr. Owen's resignation, Dr. Cart in 1951 recruited the Reverend John H. Gibson as the new director of Christian education. With his wife, Margie, and the first of their five children, he energetically involved himself in the life of Plymouth. The church school (as the Sunday school was now called) gained new vigor as graded programs from crib room through senior high replaced outmoded primary, junior, and senior departments. Veteran teachers teamed with new instructors. Among them was Margie Gibson who had attended seminary with her husband and who would for many years volunteer her services to the church school.

With the coming of the Carts and later the Gibsons, Plymouth renewed its efforts to attract new families. Ministers and members of the congregation made a point of getting to know young visitors who came to the church and often succeeded in drawing their parents and siblings into Plymouth activities. Within the church school and youth programs, Mr. Gibson promoted such offerings as parent groups, a faculty forum, sports, and musical groups. At the breakfast club newly oriented to young parents, Dean Lauer continued the popular series of Bible discussions he had started in the 1940s.

The effort to draw newcomers brought some members face to face with racist sentiments prevalent at the time. Felix and Lucy Davis had come to Seattle from the deep South and were among Plymouth members who worked on the membership drive. As chairman of the Board of Trustees, Mr. Davis frequently ushered. One Sunday, heads turned when a black woman entered the sanctuary. Mr. Davis graciously gave her his arm and ushered her to a seat. Another member of the congregation later took him to task and asked, "How could you, a southern gentleman, do that?" to which Mr. Davis replied, "Because I am a member of Plymouth Church."

The church was cordial to established black organizations. In 1948, the National Association of Colored Women had its 24th Biennial Convention in Seattle, a highlight of which was a mass meeting and tea at Plymouth. As Mr. Davis' experience previewed, however, the social changes of the coming decade would give Plymouth some rough sledding.

7
A Broader Church Community 1950–1960

The decade of the fifties was relatively prosperous in Seattle. Most people were employed, and area residents revelled in the region's natural attributes. For arm-chair adventurers, television was making its debut. These post-war years were opportune for Plymouth to widen its definitions of mission and ecumenism and to come to terms with a contemporary interpretation of social gospel.

Seattle citizens counted their blessings. The cold war with the Soviet Union and the hot war with Korea meant jobs. By 1957, The Boeing Company claimed approximately half of King County's manufacturing labor force. As further promise for a strong economic and population growth, Seattle's major employer developed the Boeing 707. This commercial jet airplane would dominate international civilian markets for years and insure the company's peacetime prosperity.

Resettlement of Displaced Persons

During the war years, Plymouth had sent packages and financial donations to relief organizations in Europe. In 1949, United Nations camps there still sheltered hundreds of thousands of people who, after surviving the Nazi holocaust, had fled their homelands in Eastern Europe. Jews and Catholics had quickly mobilized to organize an international resettlement program. Now Church World Service was appealing to the slower-moving Protestants to intensify their efforts and bring more than 700,000 displaced persons to the United States. When the Seattle Council of Churches encouraged

A hearty meal is how these former displaced persons from Latvia chose to celebrate being able to move into their own home. Plymouth sponsored Mr. and Mrs. Peter Celms; their children, Peter, Jr., and Carmen; and her parents, Mr. and Mrs. Berthold Endler, and later welcomed them as members of the church.

participation in a resettlement project for refugees, Plymouth responded.

With long-time member and community leader Kenneth Fisher as project chairman, Plymouth contracted to bring 11 families to Seattle. From the start everyone knew that the project would involve considerable expense and volunteer commitment. As a sponsoring organization the church was required to guarantee that displaced persons would have transportation from their port of entry on to Seattle, temporary room and board, and employment that did not replace another worker. In addition, the church was to ensure their welfare for the first five years.

The boards of deacons and deaconesses still had a balance of $2,600 from communion-service offerings which they contributed, and individuals came forth with additional donations. The Reverend Dr. Archie H. Hook, superintendent and minister of the Washington Congregational Christian Conference, cited Plymouth's response as a pacesetter. In a July 1949 letter to other churches, he challenged: "Every church and every Christian has a responsibility. . . . No church is too small to give an assurance of at least one family. Large churches have a larger responsibility."

In the spring of 1950, Latvian, Russian, and Polish families began their journeys from Europe by pinning "CWS" (Church World Service) buttons to their coats and boarding ocean liners. After two or three weeks on overcrowded ships, they landed in America and transferred to buses or trains to ride for more days and nights. Groups of Plymouth people were on hand to greet them when they finally reached Seattle.

The Georges, Hoys, and others took families into their homes for the first few weeks until Plymouth could find them a place of their own. Kenneth Morford and Eva George were especially active in locating temporary housing and low-cost rental homes. Evelyn Gunther headed a committee to solicit donations of food, clothing, furniture, and other basics for setting up housekeeping. Irving Smith and his employment committee successfully arranged start-up jobs. Often, the employer was someone from Plymouth and the new employee someone who did not speak English. Other parishioners helped in countless large and small ways, sometimes at the suggestion of church visitor Dorothy Purcell, who became a close friend of the former refugees.

Eventually, 10 of Plymouth's 11 families adjusted to Seattle and made it their home; the other moved to New York State to be near relatives. In a letter to the New York office of the Congregational Christian Service Committee, Mr. Fisher evaluated the project: "We can hardly believe our good fortune in having such wonderful people to deal with. They are agreeable and attractive; their attitude is absolutely perfect; they want only to work and become independent and pay back the money which has been advanced to them . . . they work hard and have given complete satisfaction to everyone for whom they have worked."

John and Nadine Poluyanow are still members of Plymouth and were among those making the journey to Seattle. After 10 days on a ship carrying 1,500 refugees, the young couple and their infant daughter arrived in New Orleans, the only people on board destined for the far-off state of Washington. From the South they travelled by train, first to New York and then westward. The $40 that they were given at the port of entry was barely enough to feed the baby, and on the long cross-country trip the parents went hungry.

Wearing their CWS buttons so that they would be recognized, the Poluyanows found several Plymouth people waiting at Seattle's Union Station to welcome them. Mrs. Poluyanow fondly recalls going to the home of William and Mabel Hoy, where the family stayed for more than three weeks. During this time, Irving Smith helped Mr. Poluyanow find a job in LeConie Stiles' bakery, and Mrs. Purcell located a small apartment and later a more suitable duplex. For the next 32 years, Mr. Poluyanow worked at the bakery to support his wife, daughter, and the two sons who were born in Seattle. He retired in 1982 to resume the artist's career he had started in his native Latvia.

While the Poluyanows and many others became part of the Plymouth family, the resettlement program was never intended to convert refugees from their own faiths. Members of the congregation who helped them wanted only to give them a fair chance. Several of the Latvians in Seattle later founded their own church to preserve their culture, and Plymouth people were supportive.

Missionary Commitments

The congregation's response to the needs of displaced persons combined traditions of service to the local community with those of missionary work in the wider field. The packages, letters, and financial donations of parishioners to missionary projects were often motivated by a deeply personal concern and attachment. The several members who over the years had become overseas missionaries wrote to friends at Plymouth about their work, the often-overwhelming needs of the people they served, and their own frustrations and achievements. These missionaries came back to Plymouth upon completion of their assignments or when on leave.

Dr. Ruth Catton had served on Plymouth's Missions Committee and was later sent by the American Board of Commissioners for Foreign Missions to a hospital in southern India. Mary Ingle came home on leave from Anatolia College in Saloniki, Greece, and induced Lakeside School's Veo Small to accept a post-retirement assignment at the school as dean of men/interim president. His wife, Ethel, agreed to take a teaching position there. Alice Gwinn served for 33 years as a teacher at Doshisha University in Japan, and Valley Nelson provided health care in war-torn Lintsing, China, prior to World War II.

Also included in the budget for missions were the International Christian University in Japan, the Education of Nationals in India, the Lloyd Lorbeer project in Pasumalia, India, and in the mid fifties, relief to refugees from Hungary. Plymouth people welcomed visiting missionaries from these and other programs as featured speakers in the pulpit, at church dinners, and in their fellowship groups and classes. Among the visitors was Dr. Frank Laubach who developed the famed Laubach literacy method and taught people throughout the world to read, thus opening doors to opportunity. His method was adopted by missionaries in schools, hospitals, and village social work and evangelism.

Winifred Herman was head of the Missions Committee in the early 1950s. She encouraged participation from all departments in the church, thereby promoting a more comprehensive program of world outreach. Mrs. Herman and her husband, Harold, had served the YMCA in India for 30 years before coming to Seattle. They invited leaders from the American Board to visit Plymouth to discuss the pressing needs and challenges of world missions. Following a series of committee meetings and negotiations, the church agreed to support a young couple commissioned by the Prudential Committee of the American Board to go to the Philippines.

In 1952, the Reverend Paul Pruitt was serving the Congregational church in Anacortes while he and his wife, Mary Margaret, awaited a missionary assignment. Earlier in the year, Plymouth had hosted their commissioning service. The congregation was happy to learn that the American Board had assigned the Pruitts to the Philippines and designated Plymouth to be their primary financial supporter.

The Reverend Paul and Mary Margaret Pruitt were supported in their missionary work in the Philippines by Plymouth. They are shown here with Filipino friends and their daughters, Janice (standing) and Cynthia (being held).

The Women's Association hosted its annual Missions Dinner with Paul and Mary Margaret Pruitt as guests of honor. An effective fund-raiser, the event was an international potpourri with each table having a different ethnic theme. Church people who had been abroad brought artifacts for decoration, and women donated their versions of exotic cuisine. The Pruitts expressed a need for a jeep to get around between primitive villages in the hilly Mindanaoan countryside. Aided by proceeds from the dinner, the Women's Association came forth with the going purchase price of $2,000.

Following the Pruitts' departure, Mr. Gibson stated in his 1952 annual report: "During the months that they were able to be with us before sailing to the Philippines, all of us discovered how we were honored through our sharing in their work. They are now our hands, our hearts, and our voices to fellow Christians thousands of miles away." From Mindanao Mr. Pruitt wrote that messages of encouragement from the congregation were a source of strength and "Not the least of our blessings is the knowledge that Plymouth people provide a large amount of our support." He told about their language studies and some of their missionary activities, again thanking the congregation for supplies that made possible such commitments as caring for the sick and for children.

Illness forced the couple to return from Mindanao three and a half years into their five-year assignment. During that time, however, they had succeeded in renewing the link between Plymouth people and their world missions. For several years the church continued to support Proculo and Eleuteria Rodriguez, another dedicated young couple who went to the Philippines as the Pruitts' replacement. Of their work the 1958 annual report says, "(They) are continuing to serve Christ there on missions of literacy and agriculture, as well as on missions of evangelism and healing."

Some Plymouth members felt a sense of loss when in 1962 the church decided to depersonalize its giving to missions and to channel a generous annual donation through Our Christian World Mission (OCWM), now called Our Church's Wider Mission. Others members were glad that the church was foresaking what they saw as a provincial outlook and participating fully in the denomination. At that time Marion Cox was serving an eight-year term on the Prudential Committee of the American Board, and Frances Owen had recently represented the American Congregational Christian Churches at the World Council of Churches Assembly in New Delhi, India.

The gradual move to OCWM began in 1953 with the pastorate of the Reverend Dr. Martin L. Goslin. He brought to Plymouth the farsighted view that the church must keep pace with Seattle's rapid emergence as an international city. By relinquishing its own missionaries and missions, the congregation was able to participate on a broader basis via the denomination's international programs. Members retained a sense of personal participation because foreign missionaries continued to visit Plymouth to share their needs and experiences and the church responded with special donations. Nationally, Plymouth quickly gained recognition for its commitment to benevolence. By size of membership and overall, the Seattle congregation repeatedly ranked among the most altruistic parishes in the denomination.

Since the American Revolution, the education of black

people had been a high-priority mission of Congregationalists. Howard University in Washington, D.C., and the majority of post-Civil War black colleges in the South were Congregational in origin. In the fifties, Plymouth helped fund outpatient services at Dillard University's Flint-Goodrich Medical School and Hospital, called in a 1958 church publication "the only hope of thousands of New Orleans Negroes for modern medical treatment and care." After his years at Plymouth, Dr. Goslin became Northwest director of the "17/76 Campaign" to raise funds and scholarships for U. S. black colleges founded by Congregationalists. His former parish responded generously with pledges totaling $64,000 in support of this mission work closer to home.

The congregation also contributed during these years to Haskell College in Kansas (then for native Americans) and to the Mandan Indians on North Dakota's Fort Berthold Reservation. In addition to giving support to Mandan churches and funding youth scholarships, fellowship groups responded in their own ways. The Women's Association donated clothing, blankets, and an oil-burning heater. Under the guidance of Associate Minister the Reverend Elizabeth McGuffie, Plymouth children established a tradition of hanging hand-knit woolens, dollar bills, and homemade gifts on a Christmas tree at the church. For several years this "mitten tree" produced more than 750 presents each holiday season for children on the reservation.

A New Minister for New Times

At the annual meeting in January 1953, members listened intently to the speaker phone that broadcast a long-distance conversation between Pastoral Search Chairman Fred Catlett and the Reverend Dr. Martin L. Goslin from the First Congregational Church in Evanston, Illinois. Dr. Goslin heard the congregation's enthusiastic response when he accepted the call, and members heard his voice directly, unlike the conversation with Chauncey Hawkins in 1920 that had required an interlocutor.

Dr. Cart had resigned in 1952 to take a pastorate at the

First Congregational Church of Winchester, Massachusetts. In the interim Mr. Gibson maintained programs, updated administrative procedures, and prodded lay leaders into taking the more active roles that the progressive Dr. Goslin would expect and that the times ahead would require.

As further preparation for the arrival of Dr. Goslin, his wife, Louise, and their five children, the trustees purchased a spacious and elegant home on Capitol Hill.* Among Louise Goslin's many church activities during her husband's pastorate, she opened the parsonage scores of times to host fellowship groups and other church gatherings.

A Biblical scholar and historian of note, Dr. Goslin soon revitalized the lecture format popular in the Fifield years. He packed the house on Wednesday nights. The young people met before dinner and then joined parents and visitors for the meal. Afterwards, they adjourned to study their school work, and the adults listened to Dr. Goslin's lectures.

The Council for Social Action

Much of the new minister's attention was directed toward an intense internal debate fueled by the fear of McCarthyism, communism, leftism, and creeping socialism prevalent at the time. At issue was Plymouth's position regarding the denomination's Council for Social Action (CSA). This debate would color the congregation's approach to social concerns and its upcoming decision about merger with the United Church of Christ.

In his 1954 account for the church archives, John F. Hall noted that the CSA was established by the denomination in 1934. It was to be an agency "for helping to make the Christian gospel more effective in society, national and world-wide, through research, education and action . . ." In the early fifties local churches began to levy various criticisms against the CSA. As a consequence, the denomination appointed a board of review to study the facts and make recommendations.

* Plymouth owned parsonages only during the Cart, Goslin, and Felible pastorates.

The Reverend Dr. Martin L. Goslin, 1953–1962

The review panel found that the CSA had given the impression of speaking for the entire denomination on highly controversial subjects. It further found all staff members to be "conscientious and sincere Christians" and rejected charges of subversion and disloyalty. The panel concluded that the CSA's primary purpose should be to "devote the principal part of its resources . . . to the education of members of the denomination and the Christian viewpoint in social issues." It also recommended a tighter rein on action programs.

Many members of the denomination felt the recommendations were not tough enough to correct the situation. In response, lay people formed the League to Uphold Congregational Principles, with Plymouth's Harry M. Robbins as a member of its board. Financed by donations, the League distributed copious literature throughout the denomination. It alleged that, under the name of social action, churches were being used as channels to advance leftist views; that CSA publications were largely political and biased toward the left; and that CSA spokesmen implied that they spoke for all Congregationalists. The League appealed to denominational leaders to reexamine the CSA staff and restate the group's purpose as providing educational information on Congregational history, polity, and principles.

In contrast to the abundant material disseminated by the League, the CSA's side was represented solely by "An Open Letter to Churches" in which the staff expressed its willingness to cooperate with the entire fellowship. The letter also pointed out some of the difficulties that the staff had faced, including trying to ascertain the denomination's position on social issues and coping with a need for additional advice, personnel, and funding.

Between the review panel's report in November 1953 and Plymouth's annual meeting the following January, members studied the issues. Discussion at the meeting centered on a resolution offered by Fred Catlett. He was an attorney who had served in almost every church office, including 20 years on the Board of Trustees. His resolution upheld the right of each Congregational church to determine for itself whatever social action it would take or approve, prohibited the CSA from taking action or pretending to speak for all, withheld benevolence funds of the church for expenses of the CSA, and called for abolition of the CSA. The resolution further stipulated that any future body the denomination might establish oriented toward social action would have to rely on special contributions of those interested, rather than on benevolence funds of the church. Finally, the resolution instructed Plymouth delegates to vote in accordance with this position at conferences to which they were delegates.

The proposal stimulated considerable discussion. One vocal member in favor of the CSA was former Conference Superintendent the Reverend Dr. Claton S. Rice. In the flux of opinions and counter-opinions, Mr. Hall quoted a prominent Plymouth member who ruefully remarked, "It's getting to the point where, if you favor this resolution, you are a reactionary and dirty capitalist and, if you oppose it, you are a fellow traveller, if not a Communist." Members voted to take Dean

Lauer's advice and adjourn the meeting until mid February to permit further study and discussion of the subject.

The second session of the annual meeting attracted a much larger gathering. Mr. Catlett presented his resolution, somewhat toned down in its aspersions but still maintaining that the CSA should be abolished. Kenneth Morford presided over the ensuing discussion wherein both liberals and conservatives had their say. A standing vote of 182 to 52 showed that the resolution had passed.

Mr. Morford received unanimous commendation for his able and impartial chairmanship of the meeting and commented: "By tonight's vote we have committed ourselves as individuals not only as being opposed to the Council for Social Action, but as willing and ready to inform ourselves on the needs for social action. . . . Having said, 'I don't want a CSA,' you have also said, 'I will not now do a Rip Van Winkle and go to sleep.' "

Dr. Goslin closed the meeting, saying that he was glad he was not responsible for the decision and that he believed members were not adequately informed on both sides of the question. He noted, however, that the privilege of self-determination was not enjoyed by other denominations and that the evening's discussion and action could only have happened in Congregational Christian churches.

Plymouth's delegation brought the resolution to district, state, and national meetings of the denomination. Each time it was defeated and at each gathering the majority voted its endorsement of the report of the review panel. Mr. Hall wrote, "Plymouth may have been the only church in the country to vote to abolish the CSA." He added, however, "The bonds of Christian fellowship in Plymouth Church were equal to the strain."

Merger With the United Church of Christ

Another source of strain surfaced in the fifties as the result of discussions started in the late forties. Representatives of the General Council of Congregational and Christian Churches and the General Synod of Evangelical and Reformed Churches were engaged in talks regarding a proposed merger into the United Church of Christ (UCC). In the wake of the social-action controversy, the question was to be hotly debated for years.

The major concern was that Evangelical and Reformed Churches were governed by a synod that had final authority over church practices. Congregationalists, on the other hand, vested this authority in the local church. In 1954, Board of Trustees Chairman Kenneth Fisher appointed a committee on Congregational polity. Its charge was three-fold: "to investigate, ascertain and report to the church what is the present relationship between Plymouth Congregational Church and the Seattle Association, the Washington Congregational Conference, the General Council and various missionary boards; to study the situation and report to the church its conclusions as to what those relationships should be; to consider and recommend to the church what steps or action, if any, should be taken by Plymouth Church to create or establish the desired relationships."

While the committee labored diligently to carry out its assignment, Mr. Catlett conducted an adult class to study the merger issue. On behalf of Plymouth, he and his legal colleague, Robert Sandall, attended conferences and wrote numerous letters to clarify whether or not the congregation's basic rights would be preserved within the UCC.

As in the case of the social-action debate, a determined lay faction in the denomination (represented at Plymouth by a small but adamant group) circulated reams of anti-merger literature. Although a clause ensuring local-church autonomy was in the merger proposal from the beginning, the issue presented ample grist for the mill of confusion and concern.

In November 1955, the question came to a vote. Plymouth members decided to oppose merger at the national level. They advised other Congregational Christian churches of this decision and requested that the General Council proceed no further with the proposed union. Plymouth then drew up an agreement with the Washington Congregational Christian Conference, wherein both parties agreed to continue to cooperate in certain programs, regardless of Plymouth's eventual relationship to the UCC.

The merger was approved at the national level in 1957,

resulting in formation of the General Synod of the United Church of Christ. At Plymouth, the painful controversy about the church's position continued. Dr. Goslin preached persuasive sermons in favor of joining the UCC. An unconvinced anti-UCC coalition circulated its literature, ultimately spending an estimated $10,000 in its campaign.

Under the leadership of Kenneth Morford and Page Ballard, other lay people organized as Members Concerned About Plymouth's Future to rally support for joining. On October 9, 1960, they sent to the membership a memorandum signed by 188 proponents, urging others to vote with them. As a basis for their stand, they cited the paragraph in the UCC constitution that begins, "The autonomy of the local church is inherent and modifiable only by its own action." Plymouth finally voted later that month to join the UCC, at which time a small group of still-adamant dissidents withdrew to form their own church.

Dr. Goslin visited other churches in the region that were in the midst of the struggle Plymouth had just resolved. In his frequent role as guest preacher, he encouraged support of the merger. Some churches acknowledged the thoroughness of Plymouth's approach to the issue by deciding to follow its lead.

Plymouth later took the occasion of the Century XXI Exposition in Seattle in 1962 to strengthen its public support of the UCC. The highly successful world's fair brought unprecedented numbers of visitors to the city. Plymouth persuaded the owner of the Monks Club on Capitol Hill to let the church have the building for the duration of the fair. Former missionaries Veo and Ethel Small turned the residence and meeting place for young professional men into an inexpensive "hotel." Until the fair closed, they managed a full house of guests from the denomination.

The Christian Witness C-21 Pavilion at the fair was funded by participating denominations. The exhibit representing Christianity's place in the world was diminutive in contrast to the magnificent Gothic arches of the federally funded U.S. Science Pavilion. It created a center for Christian activities, nonetheless, providing a spiritual emphasis among the fair's lavish scientific and materialistic displays. As part of the Christian Witness observance conducted by the UCC in

August, denominational leaders addressed overflow audiences at Plymouth. Sharing in the program were UCC President the Reverend Dr. Ben Herbster, the Reverend Abraham Akaka from Kawaiahao Church in Honolulu, and baseball great Jackie Robinson.

The merger chapter was finally closed in 1963 when the Washington-North Idaho Conference approved a regional merger. This joining of hands was literal as well as symbolic. Three years later, some 8,000 representatives of 44 local congregations, plus delegates from most of the 119 churches in the Conference, met in the Seattle Center Coliseum. Their annual meeting climaxed with the largest service ever conducted by the denomination in the region. Dr. Goslin's successor, the Reverend Dr. John Edward Felible, and Conference Minister and Superintendent Dr. Hook participated. Plymouth organist and choirmaster Edward A. Hansen directed the adult choir. The *Seattle Post-Intelligencer* called it "an enriching spiritual experience," noting the impressive and colorful bell choirs, procession of clergy, 600-member adult choir, and the children's choir of 350. In 1971, Plymouth minister the Reverend Dr. David G. Colwell would be elected to a two-year term as national UCC moderator.

Reconceptualization of Outreach

During the Goslin years, the concept of outreach as the church had known it changed considerably. From the beginning of his pastorate, Dr. Goslin took on the local legions of McCarthyites, John Birchers, and America Firsters, all of whom were seeing Communists under every bed and behind every bush. By the early 1960s, people in the community—which included Plymouth—were running scared. Under Dr. Goslin's influence, however, attitudes among Seattle Protestants gradually began to change. At Plymouth he found widespread support as key members gained new understanding of the church's liberal tradition. He notes that "The Methodists were very supportive, as were most of the Seattle clergy."

Plymouth extended itself through its greater affiliations and frequently took the lead in developing new programs.

Henry Wiegand (left) and a fellow volunteer construct a cabin at Pilgrim Firs.

Partially because of its inner-city position and its own activities, the church in recent years had not been particularly active in the Washington-North Idaho Conference. With the broadening interpretation of outreach, that involvement changed.

In line with the Conference, Plymouth in the fifties renamed its Christian Endeavor Society "Pilgrim Fellowship." The church was drawing young people from eight high schools and reached farther by hosting rallies for teen-agers from other Congregational churches throughout the area. The most popular of these educational and fellowship events were the all-city dances that attracted up to 300 young people. Within a short time youth from east and west of the Cascades were getting together for spring and fall rallies at churches such as Plymouth.

Pilgrim Firs

The Conference had no campground in western Washington, an amenity that Dr. Goslin considered vital for weekend retreats and summer camps, all of which contributed to church outreach. To this end he challenged Plymouth in the mid fifties to become the moving force in developing a camp to be named Pilgrim Firs. It was to be built on a former Christmas tree farm on the Kitsap Peninsula, a 121-acre tract with a small lake.

As chairman of the Conference's Pilgrim Firs committee, Dr. Goslin zealously promoted the project at colony meetings. He was often the featured speaker at these gatherings, sharing his wealth of knowledge about Congregationalism and his vision for the church's future. Plymouth member Julia Lane listened quietly to one of the minister's talks and later reviewed plans for the camp and visited the property. She then sent a check to the Conference for the asking price of $30,000. Her generous contribution was followed by others from Plymouth people who eventually donated more than half the funds needed to develop the camp.

In addition, members contributed thousands of hours of labor. They were joined by representatives from most other Congregational churches in the area, including some from Eastern Washington. Behind the project was Harold Herman who organized the crews that took a Saturday morning Fauntleroy ferry to get to the site for the day or all weekend. Men, women, and teen-agers paid their own transportation; but thanks primarily to Winifred Herman and to camp managers, the Reverend Eddie and Pauline Madson, lunch was on the house.

A trained architect, Dr. Goslin personally drew the master plan that guided development of Pilgrim Firs. Mr. Madson supervised construction of swimming facilities and prefabricated buildings that included a lodge and 11 cabins to accommodate approximately 150 campers. Resembling a contractor more than a man of the cloth, Dr. Goslin lent both muscle and direction to on-site work. Mr. Gibson contributed via his involvement on the Conference staff. He was away from Plymouth between 1955 and 1959 to coordinate Conference work in Christian education, which encompassed camping programs at Pilgrim Firs and at Camp N-Sid-Sen on Idaho's Lake Coeur d'Alene.

Pilgrim Firs was dedicated in July 1956. Family and youth

summer camps began, followed by young-adult sessions and weekend retreats in winter. According to Dr. Goslin, the hard work, play, and fellowship at Pilgrim Firs had an added intangible value: bringing people closer together. Plymouth members and friends have since sustained and enjoyed the camp.

Conference Expansion and Horizon House

Concurrent with Pilgrim Firs development, the Conference was experiencing a flurry of growth in line with increasing population in the region. In the late fifties its ministerial staff helped organize 10 new Congregational churches, primarily in the Columbia Basin and in rapidly expanding urban areas. Plymouth contributed to this expansion and figured prominently in the future of Eastgate Congregational Church in Bellevue by guaranteeing payment of its construction loan.

In the mid fifties, a nonprofit corporation grew out of Plymouth to pursue development of Mercer Manor, a retirement facility on a 28-acre tract on Mercer Island offered at cost by Nat and Marion Rogers. At the same time, Dr. Goslin was a member of a Conference committee with a similar objective. He was particularly concerned about older members who lived at Wesley Gardens in south Seattle, a long distance through heavy traffic from Plymouth. Their situation was typical; people had to move to retirement homes far from downtown as residential areas spread outward.

The Conference learned that Loren Baldwin, a member of University Congregational, would be willing to sell the Baldwin Apartments on Ninth Avenue and University Street. The Mercer Manor group disbanded, and Plymouth focused on supporting the Conference project. Plymouth's Bill Evenson begin contract negotiations, and Louise Kincaid launched fund-raising for what would be called Horizon House by selling her homegrown African violets after Sunday services.

The Conference adopted the project as a part of its Forward Thrust agenda, and in 1961, work crews began to adapt the building to the needs of aging residents. They constructed an annex to provide an infirmary, dining and recreational facilities, a chapel, and additional apartments. When com-

Horizon House offers retirement living near downtown.

pleted, the building offered comfortable apartments for approximately 300 residents, all of whom purchased life tenancies. In the 1980s, it was enlarged to its current 355 units.

Plymouth member and Seattle YMCA Secretary Charles Norman was the first head of the nonprofit corporation created to hold title to Horizon House. Kenneth Morford, Fred Catlett, Bill Evenson, Martin Goslin, and building superintendent Al Sanders joined him as members of the board. At Dr. Goslin's suggestion, the Women's Association purchased one of the units, and the church purchased a second one with funds from the estate of Mrs. A. H. Langdon. Both are reserved in perpetuity for members of the church selected by a confidential committee.

In his 1961 annual report Dr. Goslin wrote: "Nearly 50 of our own members have or will find a home there in years to

Father William Treacy, the Reverend Dr. Martin L. Goslin, and Rabbi Raphael Levine were the original "Challenge" team. Other Protestant clergymen participated after Dr. Goslin left Plymouth. (Courtesy KOMO/Fisher Broadcasting)

come, and this number may grow. . . . Horizon House is a rare story of God's good fortune and the faith to believe that out of little beginnings great things may come." For Plymouth, Horizon House was especially important. In addition to alleviating transportation and other problems for many older members, having the retirement home on First Hill meant the establishment of a strong colony of people near the church.

The 'Challenge' Programs

Plymouth's ecumenical development during the Goslin years extended beyond Conference activities and Protestantism. In 1960, Dr. Goslin joined Rabbi Raphael Levine and Father William Treacy in what was to be a groundbreaking venture: the weekly Sunday evening "Challenge" program on KOMO-TV. The public-affairs forum featured a Jewish rabbi, a Roman Catholic priest, and a Protestant minister discussing not only religious issues but also situations and problems confronting the troubled world. Among program titles were "Spare the Rod and Spoil the Child," "Federal Aid to Education," and "A New Year: What Does It Mean?"

Dr. Goslin said in his 1961 annual report, "Our purpose is not to minimize the differences of our respective faiths, but to emphasize the areas of common ground and morality." As unusual as the configuration of the program itself was the fact that the television station gave the religious forum a choice slot on its schedule.

When Dr. Goslin suggested the topic "Who Crucified Jesus?" for Palm Sunday, Rabbi Levine was at first stunned. The minister quickly put him at ease and paved the way for an enlightening discussion, saying, "Raph, you Jews weren't responsible for crucifying Jesus. It was the indifference of the community and of the people who ran businesses . . ." Following the program, the Anti-Defamation League of B'nai B'rith ordered 200 copies of the tape to circulate nationwide.

In mid 1962, Dr. Goslin happily announced in the *Herald* that the type of activity taking place locally was being attempted on a broader scale. A national conference on religion and race later in the year would bring together Jewish, Protestant, and Catholic groups to address the problem of racial segregation. The "Challenge" program received numerous honors, including a prestigious award from the National Congress of Christians and Jews.

As local celebrities, the three religious spokesmen were in demand to speak at conventions and other meetings. Nuns called Rabbi Levine their rabbi, and Catholic parents stopped Dr. Goslin on the street to introduce him to their children. In the community, neighbors of different faiths began to talk with one another and discover that their prejudices and fears were unfounded.

The "Challenge" speakers became close personal friends, and among their respective congregations a warm and lasting reciprocity developed. When Father Treacy's mother from Ireland was honored by the Knights of Columbus as "Mother of the Year," the three colleagues were all present. For years Rabbi Levine was a favorite guest in the Plymouth pulpit, and Dr. Goslin and his successors were often invited to Temple de Hirsch. In the seventies Father Treacy was assigned to Downtown Catholic Ministries and had an office at Plymouth where Catholics came for counseling and for daily noon-hour Mass in the Plymouth chapel. Following Dr. Goslin's departure from Plymouth in 1962, other Protestant ministers took his place on the television program.

Building Alliances

Plymouth reached out in other ways to build alliances and extend its influence locally and nationally. A Bible scholar and compelling teacher, Dr. Goslin preached sermons that motivated James and Margaret Allison to head a group of members who succeeded in getting the 11 a.m. service broadcast on KOMO Radio. Kenneth Fisher helped make the arrangements to give Plymouth an hour on statewide media every Sunday, in addition to its exposure via the "Challenge" broadcast. Many listeners subsequently called on the church for weddings, funerals, baptisms, and counseling.

Theresa Stevens continued to publish articles about Plymouth in the denomination's journal, *Advance*. As a result, the church gained widespread recognition, especially for its colony system, the congregation's exemplary commitment to benevolence, and its extensive ministry in a region little known in other parts of the country. During this period, Plymouth began to work more closely with the Urban League, Christian Friends for Racial Equality, and black churches.

In 1959, Mr. Gibson rejoined the staff as associate minister. His unswerving commitment and ability in this position and later also as business administrator contributed significantly to the direction and success of the church. As Fred Betts later observed, "It's hard to imagine the church without John."

For today's congregation imagining the church without Edward A. Hansen is also difficult. He began his long tenure as Plymouth's organist and choirmaster in 1957. After a succession of short-term and interim choir directors and organists, the church was delighted to lure the talented Mr. Hansen from Seattle First Methodist and once again to have church music of exemplary quality.

Prominent among his choristers were Margaret Myles, Sharon Andonian, Beth Paeth, Joy Rankin Newnam, and Wendell Robinson. Wally Snellenburg and Don Fleck were also mainstays. After playing humorous roles at Greenlake's Aqua Theatre on Saturday nights, they would adjust their demeanors to sing on Sunday mornings. Mr. Hansen noted in his 1960 annual report that taped concerts by the choir were being broadcast on radio.

The congregation emerged healthy from this difficult decade with strong clerical and lay leadership. These attributes would be especially important as Plymouth stepped into the demanding sixties.

8

Self-Study and Vision 1960–1970

The sixties dawned on a rapidly changing world. Technology was extending humankind's reach into space, at the same time engrained injustices were commanding down-to-earth responses. Plymouth would affirm its continuing role in downtown Seattle and, before the decade was out, take its most affirmative stand yet on the side of justice.

In 1962, Seattle hosted the Century XXI Exposition that left a lasting legacy to the community in the form of Seattle Center with its monorail, Space Needle, Pacific Science Center, Coliseum, and spaces for the arts and other activities. The city also had an enhanced self-image that gave rise to an almost-unbridled spirit of urban renewal.

At Plymouth's back door, the University of Washington's downtown property was on the verge of aggressive office and hotel development. Another major influence on the decade as far as Seattle and Plymouth were concerned was Interstate 5, the freeway that cut a wide swath through the city.

Ten years earlier Plymouth's Frank Strickland had been a member of the engineering firm responsible for building an intricate scale model of the "toll road." Initially, Plymouth's building and the Federal Court House were possible victims of the indomitable concrete ribbon. The entire congregation was relieved when Mr. Strickland reported not only that the Plymouth structure would be spared but also that the freeway would have two major exits near the church.

The Decision To Rebuild

While Seattle was revelling in its world's fair, the tides of change were rising, fed by turbulent rivers of urban and suburban growth. Spurred by Dr. Goslin's vision of what a metropolitan-wide church could do and mean in the total life of the community, Plymouth's leading boards and committees had in 1959 appointed a self-study group. It was headed by Harold Herman and was to take a serious look at Plymouth's mission.

Experts from the National Council of Churches and from the denomination reviewed church records and the building's location. Their recommendation was that Plymouth follow the national trend by selling its property and moving out of downtown. Dr. Goslin vehemently disagreed, as did many members. After further research, the self-study group concluded that the church should buck the trend because the need for a continuing liberal Protestant witness in the heart of Seattle still existed. It based its conclusion on testimony to the lasting value of the congregation's impact on Seattle, including its schools and government. An added factor was that the freeway would make Plymouth as close for its members, in terms of time, as a neighborhood church.

One of the primary concerns of the committee was the condition of the building itself, parts of which had already been condemned. The fire marshal had closed the gymnasium and top floor of the church school, declaring them unsafe for children. The structure had no proper fire escapes or exits, and every stairway was deemed a fire trap. The building had been constructed just before the introduction of reinforced concrete, and its electrical and plumbing systems were antiquated.

The ivy-covered old church was beautiful, however, and a landmark housing many memories. Despite the oversized sanctuary and inadequate church-school facilities, a vocal core of preservationists wanted to restore it. After consulting architects and wrestling with their advice, the self-study group concluded that the gymnasium under the sanctuary could not be reclaimed at any price and that the cost of rehabilitating the rest of the building would be prohibitively expensive. In addition, the group pointed out that the church needed to concern itself with parking. The automobile was not common when the facility was built. Now almost everyone had a car, and the convenience of the freeway would only increase the demand for parking.

Another factor that influenced the study was Plymouth's self-image and its projected role in the life of the community. In the mid fifties University Properties (now UNICO) assumed the lease on the Metropolitan Tract and planned to erect a modern skyscraper on the half block immediately west of the church. What photographer would be able to resist the study in contrasts offered by the stunning IBM Building standing next to the neoclassical house of worship?

Had a modernized and rehabilitated building been capable of serving the congregation and its work in the community, Plymouth might have decided to preserve it. Increasingly evident was the fact that Plymouth would need a new facility if it were to continue to attract young families and meet the future.

Members considered many and varied options, some of which resembled proposals raised in 1910 when Plymouth moved to its present location at Sixth Avenue and University Street. Like Francis Van Horn and trustees of that era, Martin Goslin and the modern board tried to interest investors in erecting an office building and integrating the church into the structure. Because no developer came forward, church officials dropped the idea.

Another possibility was to accept University Properties' offer to buy the site, enabling the congregation to move debt-free to a nearby residential neighborhood. After careful deliberation, planners overwhelmingly rejected the offer and chose to keep Plymouth in the heart of downtown. Still other options explored and rejected were trading for a site at Fifth Avenue and Seneca Street (where the Four Seasons Olympic garage now stands), trading for property across Sixth Avenue from the current site, and erecting a facility that included retirement housing.

Members did not formally decide to rebuild until more than a year after Dr. Goslin resigned, effective August 1962, to accept a pastorate in Webster Grove, Illinois. Mr. Gibson was interim executive minister, and the Reverend Dr. Vere Loper accepted the challenge to be interim senior minister.

Dr. Loper had recently retired from the First Congrega-

The IBM Building rises behind Plymouth in the early sixties. The cross from the church's copper dome was later transferred to the roof of the current chapel.

tional Church of Berkeley, California, and was a past moderator of the General Council of the Congregational Christian Churches. In his 1962 annual report, he described the scene that greeted him at Plymouth: "Wrecking equipment has leveled off buildings by the wholesale around us. The new freeway under construction is tearing up the earth in front of us, and the half block behind us is being cleared for the beautiful IBM Building." He ably perpetuated the process started by Dr. Goslin, keeping members focused on rebuilding and reminding them that they could not stand still.

The Pastoral Search Committee headed by Marion Fish Cox sought a new senior minister who had had the experience of building a church. What Plymouth wanted at this time was a minister who could stimulate and maintain a sense of community through the difficult construction period. Members voted unanimously to call the Reverend Dr. John Edward Felible from Grand Rapids, Michigan. He and his wife, Roma, and their daughter arrived in October of 1963 and moved into a parsonage on Mercer Island.

On December 4, members came together for a special meeting at which they voted to erect a new church and to conduct a capital campaign. Robert B. Hildebrand was chairman of the Building Committee. It hired Naramore, Bain, Brady & Johanson (now the NBBJ Group), the same architectural firm that had designed the IBM Building.

In April Mr. Hildebrand wrote an article for the *Herald* about his committee's interaction with architect Perry B. Johanson: "Hours have been spent talking about Plymouth's future and how it (the church) might be able to serve not only its members but also the downtown community during the next 50 years. We have discussed worship, education, fellowship, and administration needs as well as dreamt about each room that might be part of our new Plymouth." Edward Hansen as organist and choirmaster worked closely with the committee and architect because he and organ builder Herman Schlicker of New York would be designing the sanctuary and chapel organs.

Raising the Capital

A lasting contribution to the congregation was Dr. Felible's approach to fund-raising. The task had previously been considered the responsibility of the minister and Board of Trustees. For the first time in its history, Plymouth hired a professional fund-raiser, Matthew Shaw from New York, to organize a campaign that would involve the entire membership.

In April 1964, the church had its largest dinner ever, the Capital Fund Loyalty Dinner. More than 600 members gathered in the spacious Grand Ballroom of the Olympic Hotel to launch the first of what would eventually be three capital drives under the direction of Nat Rogers. Featured on the program were Harold Smith, Phoebe Jared, Dr. Thomas T. White, Dr. Glen G. Rice, and Robert Hildebrand.

Following the dinner, 16 teams set about raising funds. Franklin G. Stull and Dr. Rice co-directed these canvass

The Reverend Dr. John Edward Felible, 1963–1967

teams. They joined other Plymouth members who, through their own examples of generosity, broadened the congregation's commitment to stewardship. Within a month the canvass generated 500 pledges totaling $606,344.

With these pledges to get the project well under way, members conducted the second drive three years later. The kickoff was at the annual meeting in January 1967, again in the Olympic's Grand Ballroom. So that everyone could come, an anonymous host paid for the entire affair. Only after her husband's death many years later could Grace Smith reveal that Harold had been the mystery benefactor. As in the first fundraising drive, the congregation responded with overwhelming generosity from individuals and families to bring the total cost of the project within reach of a third drive.

Throughout the campaign, the church continued to regard benevolence as a priority. On top of their donations for a new facility, members paid their regular pledges to uphold Plymouth's commitment to mission and community service.

At the beginning of the first capital drive, members had approved a $1,850,000 budget for their new building, a budget to which the trustees and committees strictly adhered. Thanks to the efforts of Nat Rogers and Kenneth Fisher, the church arranged excellent terms with Seattle-First National Bank for $300,000 in interim financing and borrowed $90,000 from the Plymouth Endowment Fund.

Along with general and memorial cash donations, many Plymouth members contributed memorials for furnishings. Fred and Arline Betts, for example, donated the chapel organ in memory of their parents, and Nat and Marion Rogers memorialized their parents with the sanctuary organ.[1]

Prior to his departure, Dr. Goslin had emphasized the importance of ample parking for the commuter congregation and speculated that a mutually beneficial arrangement with University Properties might be the way to get it. Representatives of the Board of Trustees were able to negotiate a 42-year lease (until 2009) with University Properties whereby the corporation would operate the 90-stall garage to be constructed under the church. In exchange, Plymouth would have free use of both the Plymouth and IBM garages on Sunday mornings and reduced rates for parking in the IBM Garage on weeknights. Pacific National Bank accepted this lease as collateral for the loan to build the garage.

Bids were opened in the fall of 1965 and all were more than $400,000 over budget. The Building Committee selected the low bidder, Baugh Construction Company, as the contractor. Together with the architect, Baugh representatives patiently worked with the committee to bring specifications in line with budget. The cost was reduced by lowering the ceiling of the sanctuary, designating the chapel as an add-on if funds became available, constructing the elevator shaft without an

1. Numerous other Plymouth members have donated gifts in memory of loved ones, all of which are recorded in a book in the church foyer. The number and generosity of benefactors preclude full acknowledgment in this text.

elevator, and leaving as unfinished shells Fellowship Hall and all classrooms except those for preschool children. In joy and faith, the contract was signed. The budget for change orders during construction was restricted to $25,000, a fourth of what the architect had wanted.

During the 16 months of construction, special gifts and unexpected bequests made possible full completion of the proposed building, including the chapel. Almost at the last minute, a bequest came that was nearly the exact amount needed to install the elevator.

Merger With the Nisei

A major and memorable event took place in the old church just prior to its demolition. On Worldwide Communion Sunday in 1965, the Nisei (second-generation) fellowship of Seattle's Japanese Congregational Church formally united with Plymouth. Their moderator, the Reverend Dr. Seiichi Adachi, presented to Board of Trustees Chairman Kenneth Fisher the official records of the Nisei group, along with a check for $1,000 to purchase a cross for the new sanctuary. As a climax to the merger celebration, the entire congregation stood and sang "In Christ There Is No East or West," after which the Reverend Ai Chih Tsai, pastor of the Japanese Congregational Church, gave the benediction in Japanese.

Plymouth's relationship with the Japanese Congregational Church dates from 1907 when the International Christian Endeavor Society convened in Seattle. As a result of a Japanese rally at that convention, a group of Congregationalists came together in burgeoning "Japantown" and asked Plymouth's minister, Francis Van Horn, to help them form their own church.

Through the years the Issei (first-generation) continued to worship in Japanese. The younger Nisei, however, were quick to Americanize. Within a few decades many of them no longer spoke the tongue of their ancestors. Consequently, the church had to offer services in two languages, a requirement that meant the congregation of fewer than 150 members had to support two ministers. An added dilemma emerged in the early

Nisei Japanese Americans take their first communion as members. Serving are the Reverend Dr. John Edward Felible and the Reverend Herbert Bauck.

sixties when a city survey of the deteriorating neighborhood showed that the Japanese Congregational Church building was substandard and likely to be condemned to make way for urban renewal.

In the spring of 1964, the Japanese American congregation once again turned to Plymouth, asking if the ministerial staff might consider ways of serving the English-speaking Nisei. With the encouragement and approval of the Board of Trustees and Administrative Council, the Reverend Herbert Bauck assumed responsibility for the 11:15 A.M. service at the Japanese American church for four months. This assignment was in addition to his duties as an associate minister at Plymouth. During this time, committees and boards from both congregations further evaluated the situation.

While exploring various alternatives, Plymouth suggested

that the Japanese American congregation consider using Plymouth's new building for all of its programs. In the hope of eventually achieving a total merger of the two churches, Plymouth's Administrative Council proposed an initial integration of church-school programs and of the English-speaking Nisei at the earliest possible date. The Issei would use Plymouth's facility but continue to worship and have programs in their traditional way and maintain their own budget and minister.

The Issei and Nisei engaged in considerable soul-searching about whether to accept Plymouth's invitation or remain in a building destined to be condemned. Their church had long been critical to preserving cultural traditions and sustaining its members through periods of intense racial prejudice. In addition, it was an important liberal Christian witness in Seattle's Japanese American community.

In February 1965, Mr. Bauck submitted his written analysis of the situation to the Japanese Congregational Church. He maintained that ethnic churches were rapidly becoming outmoded and that the time had come for them to yield to the "universal nature of the Christian Church with its central message of love for all people irrespective of race or background." Although the Japanese American congregation fully accepted this basic Christian doctrine, many of its members had difficulty with the melting-pot ideology and its negation of the value of the ethnic church. Americanization had not obliterated family, cultural, and community ties for the Nisei, many of whom still bore the pain of the evacuation and internment during World War II.

Under the leadership of Mr. Tsai, the Issei recommended accepting Plymouth's invitation, thereby ensuring a strong church for younger generations. The ethnic bond was preeminent for several families, however, and they transferred to other Japanese American Protestant churches. After the historic communion celebration at Plymouth, leaders of the Japanese American church school joined Plymouth's Board of Christian Education, and children from both congregations became classmates. Mr. Tsai, his wife, Ryo, and their children were among those who chose to delay joining Plymouth until the new building was completed.

For the Nisei the next phase of the merger had its disappointing side because the older people did not follow them to Plymouth. The intimate chapel in Plymouth's new church was the setting for the Japanese American service scheduled at 11:00 A.M. Accustomed to impromptu gatherings and the ambience of their own church, the Issei found Plymouth's tight scheduling with rooms reserved weeks in advance to be too restrictive. They also felt uncomfortable about having to go to busy downtown for weekday meetings.

During this period, the city's zeal for urban renewal began to wane, and as a result, the plan to condemn the Japanese Congregational Church was dropped. In 1969, Issei Moderator Heitaro Hikida wrote to Moderator Fred Betts at Plymouth to say that, after careful consideration, the Issei had voted to remain in their old home in the Japanese-speaking community. The Issei treasurer of the Japanese American congregation told John Griswold, "Griswold san, your church is a little too flashy for us!"

Back in their own building, the Issei did much of the needed remodeling themselves. However, they were saddened by the demise of what they had always known as a multigenerational church. For the younger generations at Plymouth, the assurance of a strong and dynamic future was accompanied by a sense of ambivalence because their elders had not made the move. The Nisei could not turn back; the Japanese Congregational Church no longer offered a service in English.

The Nisei Women's Fellowship that became Circle 4 of the Plymouth Women's Association maintains close ties by hosting Issei women for Mother's Day luncheons and the traditional Japanese New Year's celebration. Through the years the circle has effectively formed a bridge between the two congregations. Its members have become involved at Plymouth and at the same time meet with the Fujinkai (Japanese women's organization) for special programs, visitations, and preservation of a valued heritage.[2]

2. For further information, see the 80-page illustrated history published by the Japanese Congregational Church in 1977 in celebration of its 70th anniversary.

Plymouth leaders and members pass under *The Sound of Music* marque into the 5th Avenue Theatre, the church's temporary sanctuary for 16 months.

A Church Without a Church Home

On February 13, 1966, a capacity congregation participated with mixed emotions in the final service in the gracious sanctuary that had been Plymouth's home for 54 years. Toward the end the entire assemblage rose and walked in solemn procession to the 5th Avenue Theatre a block and a half from the church. Heading the dramatic procession were Dr. Felible and lay leaders who bore the congregation's most symbolic artifacts. Moderator John Griswold carried the book in which the names of Plymouth members throughout its history have faithfully been recorded. Following him were Anne Anderson with the Bible, Kenneth Fisher holding the gavel, Harold and Grace Smith with the cross, and a group of deacons who guided the communion table. At the end of the parade were Mr. Gibson and the vested chancel choir singing "Forward Through the Ages."

While the old building was being razed and the new one

Church school for these third and fourth graders taught by Margie Gibson was business as usual during construction. An added attraction for them was the exciting elevator ride to and from their classroom in the Skinner Building.

constructed, Plymouth learned how to be a church without a church home. Sunday services were at 9:00 A.M. in the Horizon House chapel and at 11:00 A.M. in the opulent theater. There *The Sound of Music* enjoyed Seattle's longest single run of a motion picture during the week and on Sunday afternoons, and Plymouth had a 16-month "run" on Sunday mornings. Edward Hansen was at the grand theater organ, and each Sunday the communion table rose on the movable theater-pit platform.

Thanks to an invitation from First United Methodist, Plymouth's weekday fellowship and social activities also had appropriate facilities. In addition to helping secure the theater, University Properties provided space for the church office and church-school classes in the Skinner Building at a cost that was no greater than what Plymouth would have incurred operating the old building.

Many parishioners took starts of Plymouth ivy and purchased memorabilia at a gigantic public auction of articles from the soon-to-be-demolished building. As mementos to be integrated into the new facility, the Building Committee preserved the medallion of stained glass from the sanctuary ceiling, the three memorial windows, and the cross that crowned the copper-domed belfry. Even the granite columns that had shouldered the portico were preserved, albeit without their Ionic capitals. Civic-minded John and Anne Gould Hauberg purchased the columns and later gave them to the city. They stand across the freeway in a grassy triangle on Pike Street.

Community Concerns

In 1962, Plymouth's Administrative Council appointed a Community Concerns Committee under the leadership of Mary Skelton, a nationally known advocate of public schools and long-time member of the church. Although the congregation in the mid fifties had denounced the denomination's Council for Social Action, this committee was to fulfill a similar mission on the local level. It would help shape the thinking of Plymouth members who sought to remain active and informed participants in the rapidly changing life of the city.

Under the auspices of this committee, the church established strong alliances with other community groups and, as a result, was able to continue some cooperative service programs during its period of homelessness. One such activity was Sunday Downtowners directed by Plymouth's Elsie Sult. Participating with the church on the steering committee were representatives of nine Jewish, Catholic, and secular organizations. Starting in 1965, hundreds of older people (mostly downtown apartment dwellers) came together for fellowship, recreation, entertainment, and refreshments in a friendly atmosphere. They met initially at the YWCA, later at Plymouth, and then at the Jewish Community Center.

Plymouth's *Annual Reports* for that year noted: "This is a community service that has long been needed and one which will provide an opportunity for us to meet some who live in the immediate vicinity but who do not happen to belong to

Plymouth. Also it will enable us to work cooperatively with people of the Jewish and Catholic faiths who also assist in the leadership of the program."

Shortly before demolition of the old building, the Community Concerns Committee initiated another program. The church joined with the Indian Women's Service League to organize a native-American preschool that would emphasize parent involvement and be a model for training teachers. The church was the primary financial contributor. Because the Issei no longer needed their upstairs church-school rooms, the Japanese Congregational Church offered to house the preschool rent free. In addition, the Seattle Public Schools gave supervision and assistance through the district's family-life program.

Mr. Bauck's wife, Gen, headed the preschool's steering committee and found pupil recruitment to be the first challenge. When she and her co-workers saw native-American children in their neighborhoods, they often followed the youngsters home to make contact with the parents. Unlike the relatively new Head Start programs that required parents to bring their children to the centers, this preschool recognized that many Indian parents were either unable or unwilling to do so. As a consequence, Plymouth women provided transportation to and from morning classes. Janet Steputis was one of the volunteers prior to joining the Seattle Public Schools as a special-education teacher. She had a daily route through Ballard, Fremont, the University District, Capitol Hill, and First Hill. Between 12 and 20 children participated regularly in the program that was staffed by a paid teacher and several volunteers.

Other Plymouth members offered help and encouragement. Women's Association circles donated time and money to make Christmas jolly and to organize field trips and other outings. The senior-high Pilgrim Fellowship made 50 Christmas stockings that they filled with candy, matchbox cars, jump ropes, and other goodies. Most of the children's parents, however, did not become involved in the program as had been originally intended. When regular Head Start programs began to attract native-American children, cosponsors decided in 1968 to end the special preschool.

Award-Winning Architecture

New Plymouth rose in concert with a city-wide building boom sparked in part by completion of the freeway that spewed forth cars from two exits close to the church. Freeway Park would in later years cover a portion of the busy interstate with a canopy of green that linked Plymouth with Horizon House and other neighbors on First Hill.

A significant bit of neighborliness began with John Sullivan, a Roman Catholic whose office in the IBM Building overlooked the almost-completed structure. He expressed to his friends Kenneth Fisher and Nat Rogers an interest in making a contribution to Plymouth and offered to rally other downtown businessmen as "friends of Plymouth" to purchase the landscaping. With Mr. Gibson's help, he organized a series of invitational luncheons in Fellowship Hall to raise $8,000. The neighborly group of Roman Catholics, Jews, and Protestants included several prominent downtown names, among them Weisfield, Rosellini, and Friedlander.

For those who still had reservations about having torn down the old church, Dr. Felible's May announcement in the *Herald* was indeed heartening: "A well-earned and deserved honor came to Plymouth Church recently when Plymouth was chosen by the Central Association to receive the 1966 'New Look' Award—'for expressing faith in the future of the heart of the city and for selecting a design that will be coordinated with surrounding development to create one of Seattle's most beautiful blocks.' "

The dominant artistic touch of Plymouth's new look was the series of vertical inserts in sanctuary and chapel walls. They were created by blocks inlaid with shapes commonly seen as doves. Unlike the decending doves of Pentacost, these images are ascending. In a local economy dominated by airplane manufacturing, Plymouth's doves soar heaven-ward.

Two memorable events during 1966 had to do with cornerstones: the opening of the one from 1911 filled with cherished mementos, and the laying of the new one that included memorabilia for a future generation. The *Herald* reported that, because the new oval-shaped building had no corners, "the architects have thoughtfully provided a place of honor for our

The Reverend John H. Gibson, Phoebe Jared, Wendell Nelson, and the Reverend Dr. John Edward Felible remove the box from the 1911 cornerstone.

artifacts within the chancel at the side of the pulpit. Thus when preachers in years to come step into the pulpit at Plymouth Church, they will know that they are standing on Holy Ground."

A New Minister

After three years at Plymouth, Dr. Felible resigned in March 1967. He accepted a call to the First Congregational Church in Lawrence, Kansas, an opportunity to return to his home in the Midwest.

With the building nearing completion, the Pastoral Search Committee headed by Mr. Griswold sought an outstanding leader who shared Plymouth's vision and who would be able

John Griswold, Robert Hildebrand, Kenneth Fisher, and William Evenson set the new cornerstone in the open-air shell of the current sanctuary.

to tap the congregation's enormous potential. Frances Owen was a member of the United Church of Christ's delegation to the Consultation on Church Union that was headed by a theologically conservative social activist, the Reverend Dr. David G. Colwell of Washington, D.C. Knowing that he was ready for a change and attracted to the West Coast, she informed him of the opening at her church.

Many at Plymouth recognized Dr. Colwell as a denominational and ecumenical leader with an outstanding record of church service. Avid sports fans also remembered him as a former Yale fullback. The committee learned that he was an enthusiastic parish parson, an ardent proponent of the downtown church, and an effective participant in the complexities of urban life. In the nation's capital his church had hosted protests against the Vietnam War; he had participated in the

Catholic memorial service for President John F. Kennedy; and he had been the only white minister on the committee that planned the "March on Washington" led by the Reverend Dr. Martin Luther King, Jr. As he listened to tantalizing reports about the Seattle church from former Plymouth minister Dr. Martin Goslin, from Mrs. Owen, and from others, Dr. Colwell recognized a congregation that shared his priorities. When members extended a call, he readily accepted.

Dr. Colwell and his predecessors saw eye to eye on commitment to a host of liberal causes. He differed with them, however, in that he was to be Plymouth's first theologically conservative minister since Hugh Gordon Ross during World War I. Within Plymouth was a long history of theological diversity brought about in part by the church's many converts from other denominations. Also, the tradition of the open pulpit meant that members could either agree or disagree with the minister. When Mary Skelton commented to Dr. Colwell that his theological position was more conservative than that of most of the members, he recalls having said, "Then perhaps I shouldn't be here." She quickly countered, "No, David. That's precisely why you *should* be here."

Plymouth Enters Its Fourth Home

The congregation moved into completed areas of the building before Dr. Colwell took his post. On June 11, 1967, the crowd packed Fellowship Hall and its foyer. The choir entoned an overwhelming sentiment, singing "This is the day that the Lord hath made./Let us rejoice and be glad in it." Mr. Gibson joyfully preached the first sermon in Plymouth's fourth home. His title was "Only Wrapping Paper," emphasizing that what went on inside the package—not the facility itself—was what mattered.

During the summer, the frenetic pace of building, cleaning, and decorating continued in anticipation of gala dedication ceremonies in the fall. On Labor Day weekend a triple work crew joined Edward Hansen and organ builder Herman Schlicker to complete the massive sanctuary organ. In a news release, Mr. Schlicker described it and the smaller chapel

The Reverend Dr. David G. Colwell, 1967–1982

organ as embodying "the best principles and philosophies of the classical organ builder's art, modified and expanded to meet the requirements of the contemporary church."

When Dr. Colwell, his wife, Catherine, and their six children arrived in September, the congregation eagerly welcomed them. From the start the Colwells felt at home not only at Plymouth but also in the Puget Sound region. As a native of Colorado, Dr. Colwell loved the mountains and, along with his family, looked forward to treks in the scenic Pacific Northwest with new friends.

Heralding the grand opening of the sanctuary, the *Seattle Post-Intelligencer* proclaimed, "A new church, a new pastor and renewed determination to be 'servant church' in the 'heart of Seattle.' " For the first sermon, Dr. Colwell chose the appropriate title, "He Looked Forward." Mr. Gibson had been

The Reverend Herbert Bauck welcomes the congregation on "opening day" of the new sanctuary. The communion table was loaned by Horizon House.

church administrator during most of the planning and construction period and expressed the hope that the facility would "serve the community seven days a week."

His hope quickly became reality with full utilization of the building. The Neighborhood Youth Corporation offered programs and counseling services to provide job and skill training; the University of Washington Extension Program and Seattle Community College conducted a variety of classes; Al Anon had a support group; and the Sunday Downtowners moved from the YWCA into Fellowship Hall. With all of their affiliations, members of Plymouth drew in numerous other organizations for special meetings and events, and highly visible church programs themselves attracted many newcomers.

Another activity was geared to the hardest of the hard-core unemployed: young, developmentally limited women. The church provided its building as a laboratory for weekday housecleaning classes. Using grant funding, a sheltered workshop conducted the 10-member classes. The women trained four hours at day at Plymouth for up to seven months. Despite the extra hands, the church did not reduce its regular custodial staff during this training. Long-term custodian Richard Andrews viewed the program as a unique opportunity for service. He lists the rewards as a visible sense of accomplishment and pride on the part of participants and the chance for the women and other groups that convened in the building to get to know one another.

During September and October, celebrations were almost perpetual. All-church appreciation dinners honored the diligent work crews and thanked the many friends and neighbors who had enabled Plymouth to continue its programs during construction. From all over Seattle music lovers filled the sanctuary to hear the magnificent new organ in a series of inaugural concerts featuring internationally recognized artists Ladd Thomas, Carl Weinrich, and Plymouth's own Edward Hansen.

October began with the formal dedication. Among honored guests were UCC President the Reverend Dr. Ben Herbster, who preached the dedication sermon. At the banquet, architect Perry B. Johanson and contractor Robert Baugh presented the ceremonial keys, and Governor Daniel J. Evans made the address.

Hundredth Birthday Celebration

As the church neared its hundredth birthday, a centennial committee headed by Margaret Evenson planned a series of events. According to the centennial brochure, the celebration would "not only commemorate the accomplishments of our church during the past one-hundred years, but also inspire us to look forward to greater tasks in the second one-hundred years . . ."

The events started in September 1969. Many were scheduled on historic dates, including the organization of the Plymouth Congregational Society, the first church school, and the signing of the covenant. The traditional Thanksgiving dinner was especially significant. Leaders from the Conference were in attendance, as were representatives from each of the 17 churches that acknowledged Plymouth as their parent congregation.

On Centennial Sunday in January 1970, Plymouth had the honor of hosting the distinguished Reverend Dr. Eugene Carson Blake. He was general secretary of the World Council of Churches and considered to be one of the world's leading Protestants. Dr. Blake commemorated the signing of Plymouth's covenant by delivering the sermon at both services. Adding to the centennial festivities were visits from former senior ministers and their wives, another highly acclaimed series of organ concerts, and a centennial dinner featuring witty historical dramatizations coordinated by Richard and Margaret Heck.

In 1971, the congregation celebrated another anniversary: John Gibson's 20th year of association with Plymouth. Harold Smith wrote in his *Historical Highlights:* "At the Thanksgiving dinner, as an expression of love and appreciation, John and Margie's dream of a trip to the Holy Land was made possible by a gift from the members of Plymouth."

Starting the Second Century Free of Debt

As a lasting legacy, members launched a Centennial Fund Drive, the third and final capital campaign to retire the remaining mortgage balance of approximately $300,000 and to enter their second century once again debt-free. In a brochure describing the drive, Chairman Richard Eberharter observed: "Seldom does a church have the ability to operate in a new facility without being encumbered for years with mortgage payments, payments which cut deep into its annual budget and severely reduce its programs and capabilities."

Despite recessionary times and an unprecedented commitment to outreach, the congregation again responded with overwhelming generosity. Some older members still shuddered at the thought of the Great Depression when Dr. Fifield struggled against enormous odds to dissolve the church's lingering debt. They vowed not to repeat that experience.

Ruth Carter (left) and Isabel Heatherington team with (from left) Joseph Hall, Cliff Carter, Peter Fisher, and Eugene Heatherington to reenact a scene from the early church. Their skit was part of Plymouth's centennial dinner program.

On three occasions between 1964 and 1973, members dug into their pockets. Proceeds from the garage lease with University Properties added to the coffers. At a joyous Thanksgiving celebration in 1973, the congregation watched Harold Smith ignite the mortgage signed nine years earlier by Kenneth Fisher and John Gibson. This achievement rendered Plymouth debt-free for the fourth time in its history.

During the Fifield years, Plymouth took its first step toward ensuring the church's enduring financial health. That early endowment effort was given new life when in 1947 the trustees established the Plymouth Endowment Fund. Bequests from Mary Jacobs and Mrs. A. R. Green made up the initial principal of $800. Opening the current building provided an opportune time to bolster the fund so that its income could begin to contribute significantly to operating costs. Marion and Harold Waller and Esther and Alfred Instebo wrote letters for church-wide mailings, effectively promoting the Plymouth Endowment Fund by their personal testimony. By the end of 1987, the fund totalled more than $2 million.

In subsequent years Plymouth's record for financial giving was repeatedly one of the highest in the United Church of Christ. Despite the burden of capital drives, the every-member

Church-school representatives Kelly Strong (left) and Lael Plunkett assist (from left) Richard Eberharter, the Reverend Dr. David G. Colwell, Harold Smith, the Reverend John H. Gibson, and Kenneth Fisher at the mortgage-burning.

canvass for 1964 had yielded $120,809 in pledges, at that time the largest in Plymouth's history. The congregation now viewed its hard-won, debt-free status as an opportunity for greater service. The church took a fresh approach for the 1973 canvass: giving of a percentage of income. Stewardship leaders recognized the many other avenues now available for charitable giving and suggested that members work toward pledging at least 5 percent of net income to Plymouth.

Another boost to the operating budget came in 1980 when Mr. Gibson recommended that Plymouth make portions of its facility available to the business community at a commercial rate. Since the opening of the new building, the church had paid taxes on its income-producing parking garage. The rooms to be added to the tax rolls would include the hall now called Hildebrand Hall in tribute to Robert Hildebrand whose exemplary contributions to Plymouth had been cut short by his untimely death. Revenues from commercial rentals would increase overall income, even though they would be taxed. In addition to generating additional income, the arrangement exposed people in the building for classes, meetings, and conferences to the life of the congregation.

Attracting and Sustaining New Energy

While the building and capital-campaign committees concerned themselves with construction and finance, other committees were also hard at work. Members made knowing the city their business. On Sunday mornings teachers took their classes on field trips to acquaint students and themselves with both the strengths and frailties of their urban environment.

A program-development committee coordinated by Mary Skelton issued a 1967 report that would chart the course of Plymouth's future. Program objectives encompassed the broad areas of education, worship, and outreach and included two that clearly delineated the church's path. One was "to create a Christian community of persons who are motivated by love and concern for their fellow men, and who are committed to rendering unselfish personal and corporate service for others." The second was "to serve as the conscience of the community and stimulate it to action for the solution of its contemporary social problems."

If Plymouth were effectively to meet these objectives, it would have to attract new people. Early in Dr. Colwell's pastorate, the church used its annual retreat at the Seabeck conference grounds to consider the needs of contemporary generations and how Plymouth could best respond. An initial response to their deliberations was an advertising campaign. It encouraged people with downtown connections and interests to identify with this modern church that, unlike neighborhood churches, could involve itself in the total life of the urban community.

The congregation's commitment to its many outreach activities during the sixties was the outward manifestation of its internal strength. Plymouth people worked to maintain this strength by fostering a friendly, caring environment, despite

Bryan Bristow and Barbara Swain are among Plymouth young people preparing to hit the trail with the Reverend Dr. David G. Colwell.

the size and diversity of the membership. Dr. Colwell initiated backpacking expeditions as a means of establishing closer contact with young people. These popular outings attracted eager adult chaperones, including Richard Eberharter, Sylvia Odom, John Griswold, and Ellen Fisher. They joined their pastor in promoting summer hikes for adults as well. Fellowship groups met regularly at the church or in private homes. Over time the names and make-up of these groups have changed; but all still encourage Plymouth members and friends to develop close relationships with others from all parts of the metropolitan area.

During the sixties, Plymouth became more aggressive in responding to members in need. Part-time church visitors continued to stay in touch via phone calls and periodic visits with scores of members who were home-bound or under particular strain. These visitors sometimes arranged for assistance through other area agencies. The "Special Friend" program linking active members with those rendered inactive was instituted in the 1980s as an extension of the visitor program.

Working with the Parish Care Board, the visitation staff in 1968 began a practice of distributing to shut-ins the Christmas and Easter flowers given by members as memorials to loved

Members not able to attend Plymouth regularly enjoy fellowship and communion at the annual Palm Sunday service and tea coordinated by the Parish Care Board.

ones. With potted plants in hand, dozens of members fanned out after services to make deliveries throughout the city. Another addition to the program during this decade was the Palm Sunday afternoon communion service and tea. The church visitors and a cadre of volunteers made sure that everyone who was able could get to this touching service and reunion with old friends.

Action Groups and Task Forces

The sixties closed in tumult, wracked by the war in Southeast Asia, the war on poverty at home, the civil-rights movement, and urban crises. Some Plymouth members identified the Vietnam War as the most important issue in their lives and adamantly demanded the right to protest it within the life of the church. As a result, a discussion at the 1969 annual retreat laid the groundwork for a versatile structure for activism. It would encourage and accommodate organized response, without the entire congregation's having to be won over to a particular cause or point of view. Plymouth estab-

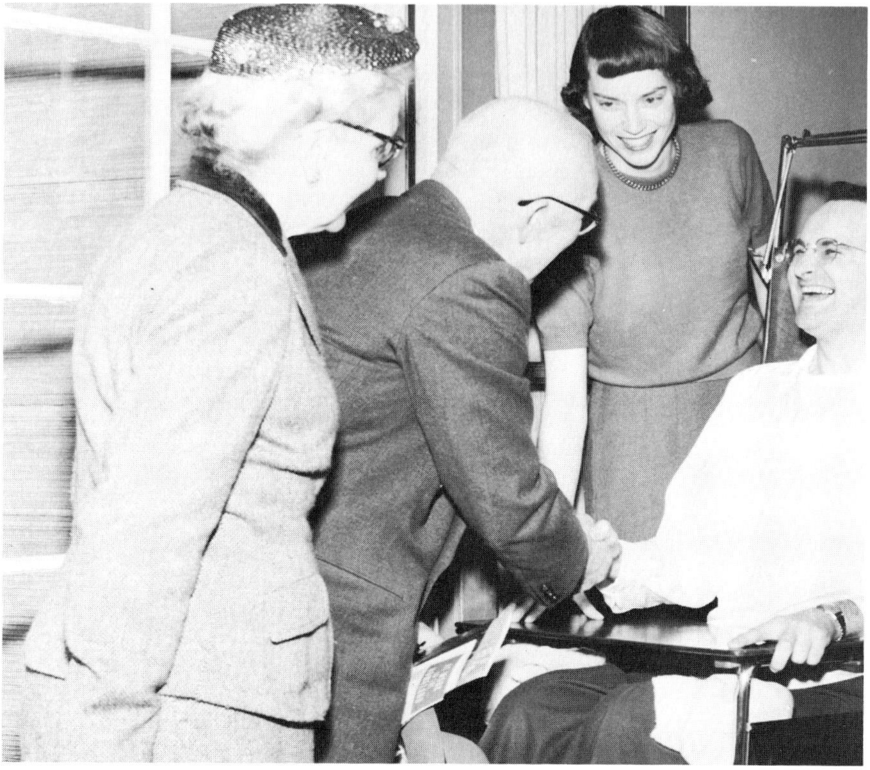

Janet and Hank Steputis welcome Plymouth callers Helen and LeConie Stiles.

lished two types of organizations toward this end. All that was required to start either was a group of like-minded people committed to a particular issue of social justice.

The first to be designed was the action group. Such an organization would be approved annually by the Church Council to pursue its stated cause. Implicit in the design was that the cause would be long-term in nature. The second organization—the task force—was devised during the seventies. It would be allied with and responsible to a board of the church and be reviewed annually. A task force was to make a concentrated, relatively short-term response to a very specific concern.

Accommodating activism within the church structure in these ways was risky because action groups and task forces had the right to come together on any side of an issue. Dr. Colwell explained: "If you're going to play the freedom game, you've got to have confidence in it . . ."

Plymouth's first test of the action-group concept was the Peace Action Group formed in 1970 following the fatal shooting by the National Guard of student anti-war protestors at Kent State University in Ohio. The group was initially headed by Hank Steputis, a dedicated church member who, because of polio, did most of his coordination work by telephone. During the height of Vietnam protests, Plymouth people would tune in television news to see 200 to 300 members of their church joining in anti-war marches that frequently culminated in Volunteer Park with Dr. Colwell as the chief speaker.

While some members of the congregation opposed this type of public demonstration, only a handful are known to have left the church because of it. During the same period, Plymouth attracted more than 200 new members. Since the end of the Vietnam War, the Peace Action Group has continued to study peace issues, advocate steps against the nuclear-arms build-up, and address the threat of war.

Toward a Racially Just Society

With their attention focused on the rapidly expanding suburbs, most residents of Seattle's predominately white community had paid little heed to the Central Area. During the fifties, the black population in that district had increased by more than 70 percent to constitute 5 percent of the city's census. In general, the white majority was oblivious to what realtors and black people knew: Seattle had developed an inner-city ghetto extending southward from Capitol Hill across Beacon Hill into the Rainier Valley. This development would become a persistent and major social factor for the city and for Plymouth.

The Reverend Dr. Martin Luther King, Jr., had gained national prominence during this period. Following the 1955 boycott of segregated buses in Montgomery, Alabama, Garfield High School invited the controversial Dr. King to speak in Seattle. Despite a flood of protests, the Seattle School Board de-

During the difficult desegregation years, Plymouth's Frances Penrose Owens and Philip B. Swain were on the Seattle School Board. Shown in 1963 are (seated from left) Bernard Reiter, Mrs. Owen, and Dr. Edward P. Palmason. Standing are (from left) Superintendent Ernest W. Campbell, Mr. Swain, Dr. Robert A. Tidwell, and Secretary Frank M. Brock. (Courtesy Seattle Public Schools Archives)

cided to permit the speech. When the local church that was to have had a reception for Dr. King backed out, Plymouth stepped forward and opened its hall for the event.

After the "March on Washington" in 1963, the civil rights movement spread rapidly throughout the country as impassioned demonstrators strove to make Dr. King's dream a reality. Plymouth people were typical in their belief that, by supporting organizations such as the Urban League, Christian Friends for Racial Equality, and the National Association of Colored Women, they were slowly but surely making progress.

Mr. Gibson had shared this outlook. In an open letter to the congregation in October 1963, however, he admitted that he had been wrong. He declared that he would stand with the "Negro clergymen" in Seattle and vowed to participate in public demonstrations for racial equality and in an appeal to Seattle's mayor and city council for open housing. Calling the cause "not only Christian, but 100% American," he invited the congregation to join him in supporting it. Mr. Gibson wrote, "If racial problems of Seattle are not solved today, *peacefully*, they might well be solved tomorrow with *bloodshed*."

While violent civil-rights demonstrations erupted in other parts of the country, Seattle in the early sixties remained calm and generally unaware that it also had a problem. Several of President Lyndon B. Johnson's Great Society projects, including the Central Area Motivation Program (CAMP) and Head Start, were making progress. At the same time Seattle voters crushed an open-housing ordinance by a two-to-one margin. In 1966, Plymouth's Community Concerns Committee asked members to donate to a united effort called "Racial Justice Now," and the committee made a point of informing itself about the work of CAMP and national civil-rights organizations.

By the mid sixties, the city was embroiled in racial tension fueled by fear, outrage, and early efforts to integrate schools and neighborhoods. Affluent inner-city districts that bordered on ethnic enclaves were in a state of turmoil as families joined the "white flight" to the suburbs, leaving behind them "For Sale" signs on homes that would be difficult to sell.

An opportunity to influence race-related decisions in city schools came in 1961 when the Seattle School Board had an opening. Mary Skelton and Frances Owen were seasoned advocates for quality education and they promoted Philip B. Swain for the slot. Ms. Skelton had been city, state, and national president of the Parent-Teacher Association and was a founder of educational station KCTS-TV. Ms. Owen was a member of the Seattle School Board, which she would serve for 22 years. She was also on the Washington State University Board of Regents for 18 years, during which time she was elected national president of the Association of Governing Boards of Universities and Colleges. Mr. Swain was at that time a Boeing executive and Plymouth's leading deacon.

He won the school-board election and went on to serve 14 successive years. He was chairman when the heated issues of school desegregation and mandatory busing reached their climax. During his tenure, Mr. Swain was also elected president of the National School Boards Association.

In 1968, Plymouth's Joint Board for Mission appointed a representative cross section of church members to make up a task force on the "Crisis in Our Metropolis." As noted by its chairman, Peter Fisher, the group was charged with considering "how Plymouth could most effectively prepare itself to help resolve those matters in the community which are paramount in creating the tensions and inequities at the heart of the crisis."

At a special all-church meeting in June, Mr. Fisher presented the task force's farsighted "Policy Statement on a Racially Just Society" that was readily adopted by those present. It read in part: "We recognize the right of each individual to an opportunity to work, to live in the neighborhood of his choice, and to enjoy the full rights, privileges, and duties of citizenship. It is therefore the purpose of Plymouth Church to work steadfastly toward bringing about the brotherhood of man."

As a first step the task force urged the Seattle City Council to adopt a proposed open-housing ordinance. Redlining and illegal racist convenants were held to by lenders, realtors, and homeowners in many parts of the city who used these practices to keep neighborhoods "white." Their rationale was that, if ethnic minorities (especially black people) moved in, home values would plummet.

The task force also promoted voluntary school transfers and officially complimented the Seattle-King County Board of Realtors for providing funds to the Garfield High School "magnet" program. When Dr. Colwell preached a sermon advocating citizen action to bring about open housing, mandatory busing, and school desegregation, Mr. Swain and Ms. Owen as Seattle School Board members publicly endorsed the church's controversial stance. In a joint statement issued in March of 1968, they said, "It would be a tragedy for the country if it were to become segregated into two peoples, one white and one black."

Within a short time the Seattle School Board adopted a likeminded policy. The hope was that, by bringing young people together in a multiracial, egalitarian setting, fear, mistrust, hatred, and misunderstanding born out of blind prejudice would fade. Advocates of this approach also hoped that, through their children, parents would find avenues of contact and cooperation that would circumvent racial barriers.

In 1972, opponents of desegregation subjected the entire school board to a recall election that resulted in a slim 51-percent vote of confidence. Mr. Swain was chairman of the board and, as such, was the opposition's favorite target. He credits Plymouth's specific support with having made a considerable difference. Corporate executives and community activists from all over the city came together in the diverse congregation to discuss the issues. As they gained a better understanding, Mr. Swain believes, they helped create a broad base of community support. In retrospect he observed, "It's hard to say what the city would have been like during that period without Plymouth." Acknowledging his "courage and resourcefulness in the finest tradition of the church," Plymouth honored him at the annual meeting as "Churchman of the Year."

Dr. Colwell's involvement with racial-justice concerns extended into leadership assignments in the broader community. Early in the seventies he headed a multiracial citizen's committee on quality integrated education. After months of weekly meetings and considerable debate, the group developed a proposal, complete with mandatory busing and magnet schools, that strongly influenced development of "The Seattle Plan." This plan enabled Seattle to become the nation's first major city to desegregate schools without a court order. The senior minister's support of civil rights reached even farther. In 1968 as a delegate to the World Council of Churches in Uppsala, Sweden, he had observed a disparity among American nominees to the prestigious central council, whereupon he withdrew his own name in favor of that of a black woman.

Further demonstrating its commitment to desegregation, Plymouth instituted pilot projects of its own. One such program provided education and guidance to unwed mothers, most of whom were black and living in the Central Area. Plymouth member Helen Karr coordinated arts-and-crafts projects in the cooperative venture between the church and the East Cherry Branch of the YWCA. From the start sponsors worked with the public schools, trying to get them to adopt the program. When the Seattle School District instituted the Teen-Age Pregnancy and Parenting School, regular curricula replaced the arts-and-crafts component. Plymouth continued to donate funds for scholarships and other uses, and women of the church contributed layettes to a number of the young mothers.

After the intensive sixties and early seventies, racial tensions eased. Issues did not, however, disappear. In the mid eighties, Plymouth's Mission and Community Service Board sanctioned a task force on racism to continue to inform and involve the congregation about ongoing and emerging concerns.

The decade ahead would bring new issues of justice and effective responses by Plymouth. It would also bring a transition to a new senior minister, change, and growth.

9
A Continuing Ministry 1970–1988

Seattle came out of the sixties with a new sense of big-cityness and metropolitanism. Plymouth emerged equipped to complete carry-over items on its social agenda and take on new ones, to be a catalyst for broad-based ecumenism, and to adjust its program in light of an increasingly diverse congregation.

The city had ambitious plans to be funded by Forward Thrust, a successful ballot issue to underwrite development of more parks, a domed stadium, a waterfront aquarium, and rapid transit. Construction dominated the downtown as skyscrapers competed for greater heights. When city officials proposed demolition of the Pike Place Market in favor of a parking lot, preservationists sounded the alarm. Seattleites responded just in time to save this unique area where since 1907 farmers and fishmongers had hawked their wares. With a newly galvanized sense of heritage, many citizens turned their attention to squalid Pioneer Square. There they restored an entire historic district of Seattle's oldest and most-neglected buildings.

Countering Poverty in Downtown Seattle

Such revitalization, coupled with other urban-renewal projects, rendered many poor people homeless. Their presence in downtown doorways and alleys was a painfully stark and visible contrast to the omnipresent signs of material progress. Adding to the numbers of homeless persons were the many former psychiatric patients for whom newly developed drugs offered an alternative to hospitalization. Institutions dis-

In the mid seventies, Plymouth nestles in Seattle's booming business district. Freeway Park, more office and hotel towers, and the Washington State Convention and Trade Center would join the neighborhood over the next decade.

charged large numbers of them to their communities where, in many cases, help was not available or sought. Like other cities, Seattle had woefully inadequate facilities to meet their needs.

With the dawning of the seventies, Seattle faced a crisis that brought homelessness and poverty to the attention of the entire community. The Boeing Company laid off 65,000 employees, a move that plunged the region into a severe recession. On the outskirts of town, a billboard read, "WILL THE LAST PERSON LEAVING SEATTLE TURN OUT THE LIGHTS."

The majority of former Boeing employees chose to stay and went to work for other companies or founded their own businesses. Seattle's resiliency proved that it had not become a company town. Many of the entrepreneurial ventures flourished. Neighborhoods rallied to help and in the process gained a renewed sense of purpose. Throughout the city people became cause-oriented, determined to survive the crisis and be better prepared in the future. Dr. Colwell observed in his 1971 annual report, "Many of us, for the first time, were actually aware of people who were hungry; few among us were left untouched by the anxiety and actuality of unemployment." Plymouth members contributed the largest special offering in church history to the newly organized food bank, Neighbors In Need.

When the congregation moved into its new building, one of its first commitments was to undertake partial support of the First Avenue Service Center. Recently founded by Fauntleroy Community Church, the nonjudgmental drop-in center was located between Union and University streets in a part of downtown that street people called home. The Reverend James T. Reynolds spearheaded the innovative program and later became a member of Plymouth.

The Service Center soon knew Plymouth as a major contributor. Dr. Colwell and later his successor, the Reverend Dr. Joseph C. Williamson, headed the board. For years Mr. Gibson took care of business and financial matters. As executive director for 16 years, Plymouth member and UCC minister the Reverend Wesley Durland coordinated numerous programs for the urban homeless and poor. They included advocacy, health services, employment counseling, a food bank, and most of all, a voluntary core group of people who cared. Other Plymouth people were part of an ecumenical coalition of supporters. Among them was octagenarian Florence Julia Robbins who became affectionately known as the "popcorn lady." She regularly walked with popcorn popper in hand from Horizon House along University Street to the center, frequently escorted the last few blocks by her constituents.

One of the mutually beneficial programs developed at Plymouth was the Youth Forum's annual Thanksgiving dinner that the senior-high group still prepares at the church and serves at the Service Center. When the program began in 1971, the group's directors were former Peace Corps volunteers Robert and Marcia Almquist. The young people insisted on scheduling the dinner on the holiday itself. They conducted fund-raising events to pay for the food, and parents helped them roast turkeys at home.

Sarah Morford Tousley's children participated in the program. She calls it "one of the best activities they have," adding, "It draws the kids together, and they grow up aware of the hard situations these people are in."

Besides presiding over the Service Center board, Dr. Colwell joined the United Way board, the Downtown Rotary, the Municipal League board, and other organizations in which business and community leaders were active. He also accepted an appointment to the mayor's commission on downtown rezoning. In a specific effort to draw public attention to concerns of the downtown poor, he was one of the organizers of the Downtown Human Services Council. Also involved was Milton Karr, long-time social-service administrator and church member. He became the council's first executive director, succeeded by Plymouth's David Newcomer.

Advocates for Low-Income Housing

In 1980, the Mission and Community Service Board created a housing task force headed by Sylvia E. Odom to explore how Plymouth might respond to the crisis of urban homelessness. Having determined that their direction would be to manage and maintain low-cost housing in the downtown area, task-force members recognized a timely opportunity when they learned that the rundown Seven Seas Hotel above the First Avenue Service Center was available for lease. The task force reorganized itself into a non-profit corporation called the Plymouth Housing Group, Inc. Although legally separate from the church, it has always been sustained by members of the congregation. Its first project was negotiation of a 10-year lease on the Seven Seas Hotel with its 30, single-room-occupancy (SRO) units.

Simply put, the facility was a mess. Ms. Odom recalled for a May 1985 issue of the *Herald* that "it had one functioning toilet, no showers, broken windows, several boarded-up rooms, many broken doors, and a few locks." Plymouth people rallied, attracting assistance from Common Ground (another housing-related agency), city block-grant funds, donations

Valerie Keim confirms that the turkey is just right for the annual Thanksgiving dinner at the First Avenue Service Center. Other Youth Forum members preparing to fill plates are (from left) Mark Sandstrom, Gene Yamashita, and (at right) Carol Reynolds. Isabel Hunt (far left) is one of the adults lending a hand.

from contractors and hardware stores, and individual contributions of household items and money.

Approximately 150 church and community volunteers joined work parties to haul trash, strip rooms, patch and paint walls, and install bathroom fixtures and carpets. Clad in their grubbiest clothes to work in the dirt and debris, volunteers made and strengthened friendships in a setting remote from their normal church and community lives. When the task was finished, the hotel was up to code and had an on-site manager. In 1982 with similar volunteer help, the Housing Group undertook rehabilitation and management of the SRO 50-unit Lewiston Hotel on First Avenue in the Denny Regrade.

Two years later the agency purchased the St. Charles Hotel at Third Avenue and James Street. In her 1984 annual report, President Edie Lackland happily noted: "Not only will 75 units be saved for low-income people, but the building's condition will be improved and its life extended." Richard Eberharter's construction company handled the major renovation, with

Ed Hansen repairs a doorway during one of the many work parties that help the Plymouth Housing Group stretch its budget for preserving low-income housing.

assistance from volunteers. They faced a deadline to win matching funds and had to schedule around the comfort of existing tenants. The volunteers worked furiously to accomplish what the group's first staff member, Nancy Smith, called an "urban barn-raising."

In 1987 under the staff leadership of Ann Schroeder, the Housing Group again added to its roster some 150 more units of low-income housing. In order to maintain that housing on a meager budget, Plymouth people continue to donate money, supplies, time, and labor. Former Moderator Philip B. Swain called the Housing Group "an outstanding example of carrying the social gospel outside the church into the community," noting that "it's made a major difference in an area of great need."

In 1981, the downtown business community organized the Seattle Housing Resources Group to preserve low-rent units in the downtown area. Among its founding directors were Plymouth members Virginia Anderson of the Cornerstone Columbia Development Company, David Colwell, and Nancy Smith, who is currently executive director. In 1986, Plymouth added to its housing-advocacy record by endorsing a successful city proposition to fund low-income units in Seattle.

Refugee Resettlement

The withdrawal of American troops from Southeast Asia was a victory for opponents of the undeclared war. As in the late forties and early fifties, Plymouth responded to the refugees created in its wake.

In 1975, President Gerald Ford announced that the United States would accept 130,000 refugees within a month's time. Andrew Hengesteg, John Griswold, and Carl Highland led the effort to organize a task force called Plymouth Resettlement of the Vietnamese. Realizing that a church such as Plymouth could provide extraordinary services, the group accepted the 27-member Hoang family that had been difficult to place elsewhere because of its size.

Hundreds of church members helped with gifts of money, clothing, toys, and all that was necessary to stock four households. Many gave their time to teach English, orient the newcomers to American ways, arrange job interviews, and take children and adults on recreational outings. As with the refugee-assistance programs of the fifties, the objective was to help these people help themselves.

Current members recall poignant moments, especially at Seattle-Tacoma International Airport when Plymouth people joined some of the Hoangs and other refugees eagerly awaiting loved ones arriving on later flights. It was a scene of tearful reunion as fractured families grew more whole. By the second year of this resettlement program, all employable adults were working, most adults were taking English lessons, and children were performing well in school.

Another part of the world embrangled in internal strife was South America. From Chile came grim reports of arrests and torture of anyone suspected of subversion and of death squads.

Ann Lawrence instructs a new American in housecleaning skills as part of the Plymouth Refugee Opportunities program.

Under the leadership of retired teacher Roberta Swartzell, Plymouth Resettlement of the Chileans was born in 1976. The group was broadly defined to include other South American countries and, with generous assistance from the congregation, sponsored four families.

In 1982, Robert Burkhart sparked interest in forming another task force. Its objective was to help Hmong and Mien refugees from Southeast Asia. They were encountering enormous cultural and linguistic barriers that rendered most of them unemployable within the U.S. government's fast-paced assimilation schedule.

Working through a refugee task force, retired teacher Robert Kirk organized a lawn-care enterprise, and fellow Plymouth member, Della Gordon, rejuvenated her housecleaning service. Both ventures were initially intended to provide employment for these new Americans, and many Plymouth households were among their customers. The task force soon realized that employment was premature; the people first needed intensive training in work habits, job skills, and English.

An independent nonprofit corporation called Plymouth Refugee Opportunities, Inc., grew out of the task force to secure and channel government grants and individual contributions into training and placement services. Plymouth members were part of the staff and core of volunteers who trained and found jobs for some 60 new Americans and assisted others in their assimilation. In 1984, the corporation dissolved in the face of sharply diminished government support, and the desire of former refugees to look after their own people. President Judy E. Pickens noted that the most pivotal factor in the decision was the group's inability to attract sufficient volunteers to an issue that had faded from the headlines.

Opportunities To Participate

These significant outreach activities were evidence of the merits of further restructuring the church's administrative organization and decision-making process. The evolution had started in the early 1950s when the church began publishing annual reports, vested board and committee leadership with lay people, and accepted the challenge to have an open budget. In 1974, members voted to give the Board of Trustees parallel status with the other task-oriented boards. It was renamed the Administration, Property, and Finance Board, and its chairman or chairwoman would continue to be corporate president.

The nominating committee adopted guidelines for terms of office that ensured sex and age equity on boards and widened participation. One guideline stipulated that only one partner in a marriage could serve on a board at any given time. These changes made possible opportunities for a variety of people to work with and learn from one another, for corporate and community leaders to share their experience with younger people, and for younger people in turn to offer the fresh perspectives of their generation.

During the seventies, Plymouth also opened church staff

positions to greater participation. Mr. Bauck resigned as an associate in 1970 and was not replaced by a full-time minister. Instead, the church began a practice of hiring part-time people for specific jobs. In addition to church visitors (who were already part-time), the payroll included various program coordinators and additional staff for the church school. The move got more people involved, tapped the skills of those best able to do the work, and resulted in a highly motivated staff that donated time and effort beyond what was expected.

Long-standing Plymouth fellowship groups took stock of themselves. In recent times the women's organization had undergone some sensitive transitions, reflecting both continuity and change. Acknowledging full participation of women in the life of the church, the Women's Association turned over management of the kitchen to the church office and in 1970 changed its name to Women's Fellowship.

For the most part, younger women no longer derived satisfaction from lives devoted primarily to voluntary service. They were increasingly entering the work force, and few could attend a daytime circle meeting, much less volunteer in the kitchen. The circles, however, were still valuable. They continued to meet regularly in neighborhoods and once a month at the church for a joint luncheon and program. The new Women's Fellowship retained the long pattern of responding to needs in both the church and the community. As in the past, its members also kept a watchful eye on church furnishings and raised funds for necessary upgrading. During Lent, the organization still sponsors the "Lenten Lectures" that Dr. Goslin had instituted in 1953 at the suggestion of Gertrude Morford.

In the mid seventies Women's Fellowship acted on Peggy Jacobsson's proposal to replace six of its regular monthly meetings with the "First Thursday" lecture series. Outstanding speakers from the Seattle area addressed a variety of subjects including business, law, education, the arts, science, and politics. The program attracted an audience of 250 to 425 each session; at least half of those attending were from outside Plymouth. These series were supported by the Carrie Raser bequest to the Women's Association and by a $1 admission fee.

The Church Council of Greater Seattle

Plymouth also had the broader community in mind when it encouraged Dr. Colwell's interest in ecumenism in the city. When he came to Seattle, he was president of the Consultation on Church Union (COCU) in which 25 million Protestants from 10 denominations were trying to find a way to unite. While at Plymouth, he remained active on the COCU board for six more years, during which time he was also moderator of the United Church of Christ. Although COCU did not fulfill his prediction of achieving the desired consolidation within a decade, it did promote a spirit of cooperation and understanding. Within the UCC, it engendered a number of reforms, including equal representation of women and stronger relationships between black and white churches.

Additional ecumenical harmony came through music. Plymouth hosted several events at the American Guild of Organists convention in 1978 at which Edward Hansen supervised competition among young musicians. He was twice elected president of the guild and was one of a select group of American organists invited to perform in West Germany.

Mirroring these national and international efforts, Plymouth played a catalytic role in fostering local ecumenical associations. Until the late sixties, Seattle churches had engaged independently in their various social-service priorities, and the Seattle Council of Churches had focused on inter-church concerns. Having lost its executive director, the Council was receptive when Dr. Colwell proposed a new orientation to create a common instrument of mission. As head of a task force on redesign, he worked with other representatives to devise a concept that was mutually acceptable to diverse local churches and that has since been emulated in other communities.

The name change to the Church Council of Greater Seattle reflected a new emphasis. Churches would continue to worship independently but would unite in a common ecumenical mission to address issues of social justice. Intrigued by the possibilities inherent in the new structure, the Reverend Dr. William B. Cate, a United Methodist from Portland, in 1970 accepted the post of president and director. At a 1982 Plym-

Priests celebrate Mass in the Plymouth sanctuary on this special occasion.

outh Forum, he said, "I look upon the Church Council of Greater Seattle as a direct shadow of Plymouth Congregational Church more than any other congregation in the Seattle area." Many members have been deeply involved in the Church Council's activities and, individually and collectively, make the largest contribution to the Church Council's annual budget.

In the spirit of ecumenism, Plymouth has since 1978 opened its building to Downtown Catholic Ministries for weekday noon Mass in the chapel and, on special days, in the sanctuary. Showing its appreciation for the Protestant church's hospitality, a group of Catholics on one St. Patrick's Day presented Dr. Colwell with a plaque inscribed "From Your Roman Flock." In 1982, Plymouth also welcomed the Korean Emmanuel Presbyterian Church. It rented the chapel on Wednesday evenings and the sanctuary on Sunday afternoons until it found more suitable quarters.

Dr. Colwell's theologically grounded commitment to social justice was the underlying motivation for his ecumenical mission. On the same basis he went to Olympia in May of 1981 to address a rally in opposition to television evangelist Jerry Falwell and his Moral Majority, a far-right group that cloaked its views in religious sanctity. The *Seattle Post-Intelligencer* published a letter praising Dr. Colwell for his action at the rally on the steps of the state capitol: "We are fortunate that at least one member of the clergy in our community has the courage and initiative to protest publicly the sinister presence of the

Rev. Jerry Falwell and his Moral Majority road show in this state. . . . (Dr. Colwell's) statement that Falwell gives religion a bad name is right on target . . ."

Dr. Colwell later explained: "My criticism of the 'New Right' is not that they think religion has something to do with public order. My criticism of Jerry Falwell is that he misuses the Bible. They almost ignore the prophetic teachings which have to do with caring for the least among us."

An Innovative Sunday Morning

A readily visible result of the 1973 annual retreat was revamping of the traditional worship format into what Dr. Colwell affectionately calls "our funny Sunday morning." Members began to see that everyone could not participate in everything and that "one size fits all" did not apply to worship experiences. For years Plymouth had had traditional worship services at 9:00 A.M. and 11:00 A.M. Realizing that a more flexible format might attract more people, Plymouth's Church Council appointed long-term YMCA executive Vernon B. Hathaway to lead a task force charged with bringing new vitality into the worship program.

The task force reaffirmed Plymouth's history of strong preaching and outstanding religious music and recommended no changes in the 11:00 A.M. sanctuary service. It suggested that the chapel service retain the popular talk-back feature initiated early in Dr. Colwell's tenure. In an effort to meet the needs of people who reject traditional forms of worship, the task force suggested adding an informal 11:20 A.M. service to be led by Mr. Gibson. The relaxed, open discussion and contemporary hymns and folksongs won an avid following. Dr. Colwell wrote in his 1973 annual report: "We have among us a far broader vision of what worship is. . . . No longer do we 'protect' certain activities as being more important than others. Rather we seek to provide a wide and full menu with the choice being left to the individual."

For some the idea of scripture, minister, music, and liturgical connection was still too confining. John Warner had promoted the 11:20 A.M. service and continued to work with

Members of the chancel choir in the mid 1980s maintain Plymouth's decades-long reputation for attracting people with the caliber of its church music.

to explore additional options. In the mid 1980s, the Worship Board started an 11:00 A.M. group discussion with lay leadership. Subjects include current social, political, and theological issues. In the late 1980s, members began scrutinizing Sunday morning again in light of changing needs and growth that was taxing space for the chapel service and for the church-school program.

Toward the end of the seventies, the Adult Education Board extended the popular Plymouth Forum so it met from 10:00 to 10:50 A.M. for a presentation and questions and reconvened at 11:00 A.M. for more questions. The Forum is yet another variation of the various lecture series that for many years have had a place on the church schedule. It continued in the seventies and eighties to draw crowds numbering 200 to 400 and to attract some of the area's most outstanding speakers on such topics as foreign affairs; cultural, educational, and religious concerns; and issues of social justice.

Transition From the Colwell Years

After 15 years as senior minister—the longest term in Plymouth history—Dr. Colwell retired in August 1982, saying, "I'm too old; it's too demanding; and the church needs a change." To make the break and to give his successor a chance to

Thomas Colwell leads a relaxed group in song during the 11:20 a.m. service.

become established, he accepted a two-year visiting professorship at the Yale School of Divinity. Reflecting on his pastorate, he told students as his alma mater: "You know, you ought to be in the parish, because I don't know anybody that's had as much freedom and as much fun as I've had."

Catherine and David Colwell returned home to Seattle in 1984 where, between interim pastorates, they are active at Plymouth. In appreciation of his past contributions and continuing participation, Plymouth's Church Council in 1987 created an honorary title, designating Dr. Colwell "Minister Emeritus."

Mr. Gibson was senior interim staff person and the Reverend Dr. Oliver Powell was interim minister during the transition year. They ably ameliorated the change in pastoral leadership and assured a smooth transition. At the same time, the church staff was undergoing other changes, including the retirement of Donna Urban who for 10 years had been office manager.

Former Seattle League of Women Voters President Ann Sandstrom coordinated the Pastoral Search Committee. Its task of conducting a nationwide search was made less formidable by the computer technology that had recently brought

The Reverend Dr. Joseph C. Williamson became Plymouth's senior minister in 1983.

the personal computer into many homes. In 1983, the committee recommended calling the Reverend Dr. Joseph C. Williamson of Boston's Church of the Covenant. Members enthusiastically concurred. Reminiscent of prior historic "calls," the congregation relayed its exuberance via speaker phone to the new minister and his wife, Donna DiSciullo, who had both stayed up until nearly midnight awaiting word. In modern times the technique remains dramatic, with no loss of its bonding appeal.

A self-professed urban minister who finds the complexities and challenges of the city invigorating, Dr. Williamson was attracted by Plymouth's varied membership and its commitment to social responsibility. Like his predecessor, he also relished the region's capitivating natural attributes. With his wife, the youngest of his three sons, and her two daughters,

Dr. Williamson moved to Seattle where he began his pastorate in September 1983.

Sexual Equity and Feminist Theology

In Boston Dr. Williamson and a woman had shared the pulpit as equals. His commitment to the justice of sexual equity was further evidenced by his support of Ms. DiSciullo's decision to be ordained in 1986 and hold a pastorate in the Unitarian Universalist Church. Feminists within Plymouth welcomed the encouragement of the new minister in the process of understanding the sometimes-obvious and sometimes-subliminal issues around sexual justice.

Prior to the women's movement that surfaced in the late 1960s, Plymouth had already made perceptible changes. Sex-segregated classes and fellowship groups were a thing of the past by the early 1950s. During the Goslin pastorate, the Reverend Elizabeth McGuffie was responsible for the church school and parish visitation. Linking her hiring with the contemporary political movement for women's rights would be wrong, however. Dr. Goslin's view was that "She was a person that could do a good job. The fact that she was a woman didn't make any difference."

During the same period, other women were claiming leadership roles. By the time he wrote his 1973 annual report, Dr. Colwell was able to state: "Women have served in all offices, have ushered and served communion among us. I'm sure that you have noticed in 1973 all of our major office holders were women: Marion Waller, Moderator, and the Chairpersons (we really have to learn to say it that way, I think) of each of our major boards: Helen Boyd, Deacons, Ann Sandstrom, Trustees; Roberta Swartzell, Joint Board for Mission; Peggy Jacobsson, Adult Education; Ruth Kiemle, Children and Youth. I say great! I also affirm that we've never had a better year than we have had with these leaders steering us."

While achieving parity in lay administration, some Plymouth women early in the Williamson pastorate emphasized the disavowal of equality implied by traditional ecclesiastical language. The problem had for some time also concerned the

Worship Board. In 1986, the church adopted a policy of inclusive language that extends to music and official church communications. The preamble reads in part: "The policy of Plymouth Congregational Church is to support and reflect equal opportunity for and sensitivity to all, without discrimination because of race, color, religion, sex, national origin, disability, age, or sexual orientation . . . to create an atmosphere conducive to the full participation of all."

Another decision of the mid eighties was to expand the ministerial staff in order better to serve the church school and to develop small-group activities within the congregation. The time was also opportune to diversify the staff. In April 1986, Plymouth welcomed as a new associate minister the Reverend Elizabeth N. Oettinger from Duluth, Minnesota. With her were her architect husband, Charles Gerke, and their two young daughters. She came as a strong preacher with her own set of metaphors stemming from her experience as a young woman. Unlike a long line of Plymouth pastors who have implored members to "block the kick" of injustice or "carry the ball" of advocacy, she includes images associated with motherhood and the home.

Just before Ms. Oettinger's arrival, some women at Plymouth formed the Feminist Theology Group. It is allied with Women's Fellowship and meets for regular study and special retreats.

Ministering to Families

An intrinsic quality of Plymouth is its historic emphasis on ministering to families, a fact that Seattle's rapid urban development and consequent spread to the suburbs has not altered. Children and youth profit from a church-school program that in 1970 began employing salaried staff coordinators for preschool through senior high. This plan enables the church to attract and retain outstanding professionals who are responsible for preparatory tasks. A cadre of volunteers now numbering nearly 80 assists on Sunday mornings. On Youth Sunday when the high-school group conducts two services and in numerous outreach programs starting at an early age,

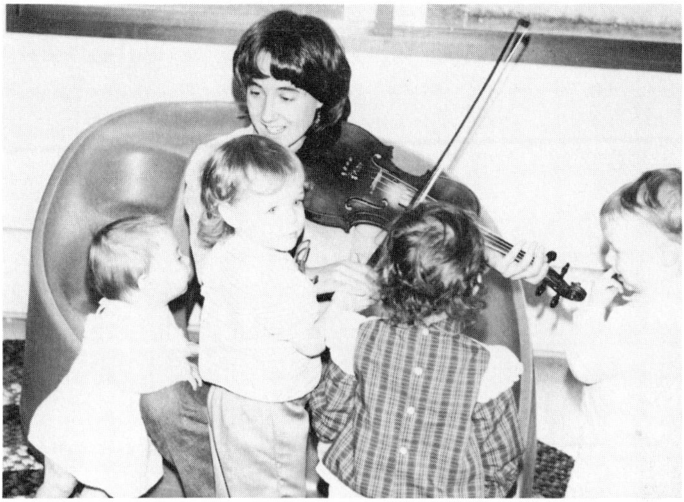

Seattle Infant Development Center staff member Ann Michael shares her musical talents with these curious toddlers.

young people are drawn into the mainstream of church activity and into the complexities of the urban environment.

Today, single- and two-parent families, couples without children, and single adults mingle on an equal footing. In response to these diverse family structures, Plymouth has in recent years made child care integral to church-wide events. Parents attending weekend retreats have the option of deducting child-care costs from registration fees. The annual family camp at Camp N-Sid-Sen on Lake Coeur d'Alene is organized so that families of all configurations can afford to go and can participate fully. Some at Plymouth may still bat an eye at "nontraditional" family arrangements; others, however, rally to their support.

Long sensitive to child-care needs of working parents, Plymouth in 1979 leased four church-school rooms, an auxiliary kitchen, and an outdoor play area to the Seattle Infant Development Center, a separate nonprofit day-care program. CBS Television featured the program as the first downtown infant center in any major American city. On weekdays parents who work downtown bring their infants and toddlers to Plymouth for professional care and early preschool education. The downtown location means that parents can spend time during work breaks with their children and during the commute to and from home.

New Directions

In 1966, Congress established the National Endowment for the Arts and the following year the King County Arts Commission became the first publicly funded arts agency in the country. Since then, the burgeoning of public art—along with big-league sports—has been as dramatic in Seattle as anywhere in the country. At Plymouth organist and choir director, Edward Hansen has for more than 30 years coordinated a highly acclaimed program of modern and traditional church music. During this time, the church has offered numerous free concerts to the public, including the year-round weekly organ recitals at noon on Wednesdays that attract downtown people for music and respite from the pace of the day.

Dr. Williamson brought a vision of an expanded arts program that has found support among members, several of whom are active in city cultural organizations. In 1985, the church launched an annual arts festival that integrates the creative talents of members, friends, and outside artists into worship services, the Plymouth Forum, and other weekend activities. Women's Fellowship partially underwrites the celebration and has also established a circle devoted to playreading.

The spirit of internationalism evident in the seventies has continued. In the interest of world peace and intercultural understanding, Seattle has reached out to many parts of the world to forge "sister city" relationships. Frequently, these cities are in strife-ridden countries or where bonds with the United States government are at best tenuous. By 1983, political upheaval was close to home, giving rise at Plymouth to the Central American Task Force. In addition to being a conduit for political activism, it was established as a way to identify and promote Plymouth's direct assistance in the region.

Following a tour of the area sponsored by the United Church of Christ, Plymouth member and retired UCC minister the Reverend Paul Sutley successfully promoted a

Plymouth Organist and Choir Director Edward Hansen plays the Schlicker organ shortly after it was installed.

brother-sister church relationship with Iglesia Morava, a Moravian congregation in Managua, Nicaragua. Under the leadership of Janet Steputis, a church-wide representative committee organized appropriate activities. Among those have been exchange visits, financial support for construction of an education wing for the Managua church, and donations of educational supplies by the church school.

Several Plymouth people have visited Central American countries under this and other auspices to look, listen, and advocate human rights. They have brought back first-hand information about complex political calamities, injustice, heroic humanitarian efforts, and ways that Plymouth could help. As a result, the congregation has made special donations, including a badly needed generator to a UCC clinic in Honduras and funds for an orphanage in El Salvador.

Under the leadership of William Gremley, the task force also got involved in the sanctuary movement. Within the church, it encouraged members to support a city council resolution to declare Seattle a sanctuary city for Central American "refugees" denied legal entry into this country. Ultimately, Seattle voters rejected sanctuary status. On July 4, 1986, as the nation celebrated the 100th birthday of the Statue of Liberty, Plymouth hosted an emotional inter-faith service attended by Salvadorans sheltered in other churches. A banner in front of the church read, "Give me your huddled masses, yearning to be free," and Dr. Williamson told the Central Americans that the sanctuary movement welcomed them, even though the government did not.

Despite the stance of the city and task force in favor of sanctuary, other vocal members of the congregation decried flaunting of immigration laws. While sympathizing with the plight of those driven from their homelands, some favored trying to amend the laws via the democratic process rather than openly defying them. Thus, Plymouth has not taken a formal position on the issue. The group continues to study, to work with other community groups, and to keep the congregation informed and involved.

Liberal Witness in the Heart of the City

Like Seattle, Plymouth in its history has gone through action-oriented periods followed by pauses to reflect and regroup. This account has attempted to capture both actions and pauses. Today, the church is again in a reflective phase, scrutinizing the human face of the city to identify where it can make a difference. A study/education group focusing on the complexities of tax reform in the state is a recent social-action initiative of members. The Plymouth AIDS Task Force is working through the Parish Care Board to address concerns related to the deadly acquired immune deficiency syndrome epidemic and to the church's relationship with its homosexual and bisexual constituency.

Advertising, direct mail, and media relations supplement person-to-person communication to let prospective members know about Plymouth's metropolitan ministry. "This bus goes to Plymouth" was an eye-catcher in the early 1980s.

Like his predecessors, Dr. Williamson takes seriously his role as a leader charged with learning from history and channeling the energies generated by Plymouth's multiple dynamics into a pathfinding vision. Aptly, he reminds the congregation of its legacy and the risk of moving into the future with purpose: "If we do not take that risk, then we are no longer Plymouth Church but a shadow of that identity that has shaped the continuing character of this people."

Internally, the congregation's spiritual life, fellowship, study of public issues, and decision-making processes sustain members and strengthen their resolve. Externally, they work to make a difference against the backdrop of nuclear arms, fragile world affairs, and lingering prejudice. As in the past, the church seeks to direct its energies into issues of social justice—advocating change and extending a helping hand. In this spirit Plymouth enters its thirteenth decade, the open, caring fellowship of a strong downtown church with a metropolitan ministry.

Appendix

Covenants

The following covenant of the First Congregational Church of San Francisco was used at the founding meeting of Plymouth Congregational Church in 1870:

You do now in the presence of God, the searcher of hearts, and before angels and men, avow the Lord Jehovah to be your God, loving the Father as your Father, trusting in his son Jesus Christ as your Savior, and welcoming the Holy Spirit at your Comforter and Sanctifier.

Professing true sorrow for your sins, and renouncing them forever, you do now publicly devote yourself to God, promising to walk before Him in obedience and love all your future life.

You do cheerfully and heartily promise that in the sanctuary, in the family, and in the closet, and in every situation and relation of life, you will be a true disciple of Christ, and by the discharge of all your public and private duties commend His gospel to the world.

You moreover covenant that you will walk with this church in all the ordinances of the Gospel, in the attendance upon its meetings for prayer, its public worship and its Sacraments, in love and charity with its members, conscientiously laboring to promote its purity, peace, union and edification.

Humbly relying on the help of God, you thus covenant and promise.

The covenant used today:

We covenant with one another to seek and to respond to the Word and the will of God. We propose to walk together in God's ways, made known and to be made known to us. We hold it to be the mission of the Church to witness to the Good News of God made known to us in Jesus Christ and to strive for truth, for justice, and for peace. As did our forebears, we depend upon the Holy Spirit to lead and to empower us. We pray for the coming of God's Peace, and we look with faith to the triumph of righteousness and life.

Senior Ministers

1869–1872	John F. Damon
1873–1874	Norman McLeod
1875–1876	James Hall
1876–1883	J. F. Ellis
1884	Frank Taylor
1884–1889	Henry L. Bates
1889–1891	George A. Tewksbury
1891–1895	Wallace Nutting
1895–1905	W. H. G. Temple
1906–1914	Francis Van Horn
1915–1918	Hugh Gordon Ross
1921–1927	Chauncey J. Hawkins
1927–1941	L. Wendell Fifield
1942–1946	Allan I. Lorimer
1947–1952	Dwight L. Cart
1953–1962	Martin L. Goslin
1963–1967	John Edward Felible
1967–1982	David G. Colwell
1983–	Joseph C. Williamson

Officials of the Church

These people have been Plymouth's principal officials during the past four decades. The names of earlier ones are obscured in church records.

	Chairman, Board of Trustees, and Corporate President	**Moderator**
1947	Fred A. Burwell	
1948	Fred W. Catlett	
1949	James F. Blanchard	Kenneth R. Fisher
1950	Felix M. Davis	Fred W. Catlett
1951	Felix M. Davis	Robert Sandall
1952	R. Mort Frayn	Edward H. Lauer
1953	William E. Evenson	Kenneth J. Morford
1954	Kenneth R. Fisher	Claton S. Rice
1955	Kenneth R. Fisher	Charles G. Norman
1956	William E. Hoy	Felix M. Davis
1957	George F. Shindler	William E. Evenson
1958	George F. Shindler	Otis E. Hancock
1959	R. Mort Frayn	Charles L. Burton
1960	R. E. "Dick" Cady	Fred W. Catlett
1961	Frederick V. Betts	Thomas T. White
1962	Page H. Ballard	R. I. Rowe
1963	Page H. Ballard	M. M. Ballard
1964	Kenneth R. Fisher	William Wesselhoeft
1965	Kenneth R. Fisher	Page H. Ballard
1966	Kenneth R. Fisher	John W. Griswold
1967	Kenneth R. Fisher	William E. Evenson
1968	Marion J. Waller	Clifford W. Carter
1969	Thomas T. White	Frederick V. Betts

1970	Thomas T. White	Robert B. Hildebrand
1971	Joseph W. Hall	Richard L. Eberharter
1972	Joseph W. Hall	Alan Bushley
1973	Ann Sandstrom	Marion J. Waller
	Chairperson, Administration, Property, and Finance Board, and Corporate President	**Moderator**
1974	Joseph W. Hall	Franklin G. Stull
1975	Starr M. Hashiguchi	Franklin G. Stull
1976	Shirley Cartwright	Russell F. Tousley
1977	David A. Bennett	Russell F. Tousley
1978	Betty J. Eberharter	Howard Reynolds
1979	Betty J. Eberharter	Howard Reynolds
1980	William L. Ean	Ann Sandstrom
1981	William L. Ean	Ann Sandstrom
1982	Jeanne Reynolds	Russell F. Tousley
1983	Jeanne Reynolds	Russell F. Tousley
1984	Sarah Tousley	Philip B. Swain
1985	Michael C. Hayden	Philip B. Swain
1986	Michael C. Hayden	Robert Burkhart
1987	Richard I. Sedgley	Robert Burkhart
1988	Richard I. Sedgley	Nancy F. Smith

Presidents of the Women's Association and Women's Fellowship

The following women served, in order, from 1907 to 1939 and were known at the time by the husband's name. When available, their own names are included. Prior to 1907, the organization was called Ladies' Aid Society. Its name was changed in 1970 from Women's Association to Women's Fellowship.

Mrs. John (Serina Olive) Schram
Mrs. W. H. (Clara) Flett
Mrs. Alfred Williams
Mrs. Everett (Mary D.) Smith
Mrs. T. J. (Anna F.) Pennell
Mrs. Henry Pennock
Mrs. H. A. (May W.) Raser
Mrs. J. F. (Carrie L.) Pike
Mrs. F. E. B. Smith
Mrs. A. E. (Alice E.) Rayner
Mrs. W. P. (Evangeline A.) Harper
Mrs. E. B. (Lucy L.) Burwell
Mrs. Fred W. (Florence) Catlett
Mrs. C. H. (Clara) Eckart
Mrs. Dan (Muriel B.) Earle
Mrs. H. W. (Lena) Yuile
Mrs. Anthony Cales
Mrs. Edward H. (Edna) Lauer
Mrs. J. G. (Roma H.) Pritchard

Presidents since 1939:

1939–1941	Elizabeth Burwell
1941–1943	Helen D. Stiles
1943–1945	Ann Hall
1945–1947	Phoebe B. Jared
1947–1949	Margaret Hills
1949–1951	Ella R. Uden
1951–1952	Marion Collarino
1952–1954	Lucile F. Davis
1954–1955	Evelyn L. Gunther
1956	Marion Cross
1956–1958	Gertrude M. Woodcock
1958–1960	Nellie Gilkerson
1960–1962	Phoebe B. Jared

1962–1964	Helen Lilygren
1964–1966	Myrna Estes
1966–1968	Mary Copeland
1968	Phoebe B. Jared
1969	Grace Sherry
1970–1972	Elsie Sult
1972–1974	Jane I. Hall
1974–1976	Mary Wright
1976–1978	Ruby Davis
1978–1980	Frances P. Owen
1980–1982	Roberta Swartzell
1982–1984	Marceline Erlandson
1984–1986	Marlene Falkenbury
1986–1988	Catherine Colwell

Recipients of the Annual Plymouth Award

Plymouth established its annual awards program in 1963 to recognize long-term contributions of lay members to the church and community. The awards are given for service within Plymouth that is a model of loving concern for others, for leadership within the church, and for leadership within the community. All awardees are grouped on the following list:

1963	Page H. Ballard
1964	Harold V. Smith
1965	Kenneth R. Fisher Mary Skelton
1966	Robert B. Hildebrand Phoebe B. Jared
1967	William E. Evenson Eva M. George
1968	Henry W. Steputis Janet R. Steputis
1969	Mary P. Copeland Richard L. Eberharter John W. Griswold
1970	Anne G. Anderson Charles L. Burton
1971	Roberta Swartzell Thomas T. White
1972	Seiichi Adachi Ann Sandstrom George F. Shindler Elsie Sult
1973	Richard Heck Mary E. Wright

1974	Delia Bergstrom Eleonora Bergstrom Helen Boyd Clarice Clemons R. Mort Frayn Frances Penrose Owen Marion J. Waller
1975	Marion Fish Cox Andrew T. Hengesteg Nancy A. Schoettler Clifford Skelton Franklin G. Stull Philip B. Swain Russell F. Tousley
1976	Dorothy Brennan Lillian Campbell Vernon B. Hathaway Peggy Anne Jacobsson Emmet A. Ogle Frances White Dorothy Wilcox
1977	David A. Bennett Alfred C. Instebo Basil J. Mitchell Florence W. Robbins Nat S. Rogers Alene M. Willett
1978	Bernice Cudhie Donald Schuman Grace Smith Helen D. Strickland Harold E. Willard
1979	Arline E. Betts Frederick V. Betts Charles L. Burton Denny Burton Jeanne Epp Esther Kinney Kenneth Kinney Howard Reynolds

1980	George A. Daum Margaret A. Gibson Sylvia E. Odom
1981	Plymouth Housing Group: Marcia M. Almquist Virginia Anderson William N. Appel David G. Colwell George A. Daum Richard L. Eberharter Edie Lackland Richard C. Locke Timothy A. Manring Sylvia E. Odom Jeanne C. Reynolds Nancy F. Smith
1982	Harriet Gruger Catherine Howze Charles Howze John D. Warner
1983	Thomas M. Colwell Robert Kirk Jeanne C. Reynolds
1984	Robert Burkhart Marceline Erlandson Cynthia Grund Warren Smith
1985	Anita Gras Bryant David Gaines Milton Karr Shirley Reiss
1986	Karen Gwilym Don Gwilym Barbara White
1987	Robert Almquist Hedy Fredrickson Phil Fredrickson Carol Sowdon

Index

About the Author

Mildred Tanner Andrews has a doctorate in German from the University of Washington. A native of Seattle, she has a fascination with the character of the people and organizations that helped shape this dynamic community. Her books include *Seattle Women: A Legacy of Community Development* and *Washington Women as Path Breakers*, both of which are pioneering studies that infuse the much-neglected role of women's associations into area history.